# Stop Politically
# Driven Education

# Stop Politically Driven Education

## Subverting the System to Build a New School Model

Eldon "Cap" Lee

Foreword by Deborah Meier

ROWMAN & LITTLEFIELD
*Lanham • Boulder • New York • London*

Published by Rowman & Littlefield
An imprint of The Rowman & Littlefield Publishing Group, Inc.
4501 Forbes Boulevard, Suite 200, Lanham, Maryland 20706
www.rowman.com

6 Tinworth Street, London SE11 5AL, United Kingdom

British Library Cataloguing in Publication Information Available

**Library of Congress Cataloging-in-Publication Data**

Names: Lee, Eldon, 1942- author.
Title: Stop politically driven education : subverting the system to build a new
   school model / Eldon "Cap" Lee ; foreword by Deborah Meier.
Description: Lanham, Maryland : Rowman & Littlefield, 2019. | Includes
   bibliographical references and index.
Identifiers: LCCN 2018043442 (print) | LCCN 2018055455 (ebook) |
   ISBN 9781475848632 (electronic) | ISBN 9781475848625 (pbk. : alk. paper)
Subjects: LCSH: Educational change—United States. | Education—Aims and
   objectives—United States. | School improvement programs—United States.
Classification: LCC LA217.2 (ebook) | LCC LA217.2 .L437 2019 (print) |
   DDC 371.2/07—dc23
LC record available at https://lccn.loc.gov/2018043442

♾️™ The paper used in this publication meets the minimum requirements of American National Standard for Information Sciences—Permanence of Paper for Printed Library Materials, ANSI/NISO Z39.48-1992.

Printed in the United States of America

*I dedicate this book to my daughter*
*Victoria C. Lee*
*The love of my life*

# Contents

# Foreword

I've spent the past half century both cheering and booing American public schooling. As a parent of three children attending first Chicago, then Philadelphia, and finally New York City public schools, I was alternately happy and infuriatingly sad. As a public school teacher, who was working in the same system my children attended, I was full of pride and admiration for my colleagues one day and full of frustration the next, particularly due to the unequal treatment of our children.

We were stuck, a hundred or more years ago, within a system designed to prepare a small number of white children with the knowledge and disposition to be the rulers—the deciders-of very complicated national interests. It was sufficient to provide others—the rest of the white Americans with basic literacy and numeracy. Meanwhile, for children of color there were little or no expectations!

As educators, a hundred years later, we are being judged on our ability to accomplish the very different task of providing a ruling class education for all students while still trapped in the same antiquated system. Under these circumstances, how can I not be generous in thinking about my colleagues caught in the middle of this paradox? I was one of them after all. We were set up to fail. And an accountability system was even designed (standardized testing) to guaranty large scale failure.

But like Cap Lee, I couldn't let go. In part because the children I taught were so fascinating I found myself becoming wiser in their presence. In part also because, as I struggled to become an ally and family friend, I grew amazed at how well most families found ways to do their best for their children. And because, in the end, I figured out ways to create public schools where we all enjoyed being together, working tirelessly to overcome the odds presented by our school system, while also doing what Cap has described in this book. Here he is spreading the word about those possibilities while also taking note of why it shouldn't be so very hard to do.

Above all, we intend to educate a whole generation to preserve and nourish a democracy where everyone is a member of "the ruling class."

Thanks, Cap.

Deborah Meier

# Preface

On these pages is a call to action for teachers who have been shackled by the self-serving motives of the agenda driven politicians. Here we present a new innovative process designed to prepare children to be productive members of their community from appreciating the role of the arts to recognizing the many needs they must have to thrive daily. Students are empowered to take charge of their educational lives where thinking is valued above obedience and children are free to grow.

The greatest challenge to educators in this decade is to prepare children to rise above the confirmation bias and embrace critical thinking. Too often our tendencies are to believe everything we hear without question. In this day of fake information, everything requires in depth thinking, research, and processing.

The time has come to go underground to subvert the system from the bottom up, assuring children the quality education they deserve. We infuse creative ideas where they go unnoticed by the politicians. We provide a pattern for systemic change that empowers teachers with a step by step approach to whole child reform allowing them to take back their profession in a clandestine manner. We empower students to unleash the genius inside all of them and parents to be full partners in the process.

It is once again time to protect children from those politicians who are adamant in their desire to keep them in their place. Teachers are the saviors who are in the position to expand children's minds to the stars and beyond, once again giving them hope that they will make the world a better place for all. It is time to take a risk for children, by subverting the system for the goal of true, whole child education. If not now, when?

# Acknowledgments

Deborah Meier for her expert advice and support.

Victoria Lee for editing the book.

Mary Gale Budzisz who supplied lesson plans for this book and much more.

Luz Estela Narvaez por su apoyo incondicional.

Dr. Angela Dye without whom I would have never gotten this far.

Catherine Spivey, Cal Adams, Donna Yates Mace, Debi Chittenden Harris-Owens, Dr. LaShawn Roscoe Scott, and Ranjit Singh for taking their precious time to muddle through my drafts.

And every student I had contact with because they taught me so much.

*Chapter 1*

# What Have We Done to Our Children?

Welcome to today's world of education where all the women are expected to be ten's, all the men to be scientists and all the children better be above average on the huge test. This is an educational world that treats children like objects rather than subjects. A world that doubles down on a failed system of education where doing damage to the least of them is accepted as everyday business. A system of education where the first go to college and the last are thrown into the streets like rubbish.

Educational leaders still believe that scoring well on a test is an indicator of how students can function in the university, or in life and the way to achieve this is to sit for a longer time in a classroom until they "get it." Why waste time on recess, the arts, home economics, and industrial education when children can be involved in developing grit? And they better do it all at the same time, in the same class, in the same seat, thinking the same, learning the same, walking the same, talking the same on the same scripted test with the same scripted answers.

With the complexity of today's society, children will no longer succeed simply by muddling their way through an outdated education system. Nor will they have the tools to succeed by simply consuming meaningless data or spending valuable time re-learning what they already know. Memorizing facts leads to information gathered and quickly forgotten as they move into the needs of the real world. Simply answering someone else's questions with condensed responses rarely leads to exploration and deep thinking. Too many schools today continue the practices of yesterday, designed to bolster the elite while forcing the rest into oblivion, struggling for survival.

## TRAPPED IN AN ENTRENCHED SYSTEM

The current, archaic system of education is so entrenched that even advocates for children are fighting to force unwitting students into a tiny, contrived box full of word games and math riddles. "All students can learn" is the motto used by many, but what are they learning? Are they learning to respond or are they learning to think? Are they learning to read or are they challenging everything they read to make sense of it?

> *"Don't just teach your children to read . . . teach them to question what they read. Teach them to question everything."* —George Carlin

Although well intended, these advocates are leading children down a path that is failing for those who are said to be succeeding. A path where success on the test trumps critical, rational thinking leaving children to fend for themselves when they awaken in the real world. The current system is a "set-up" designed to promote those who have developed the ability to respond at a certain rate and manner while "pushing-out" those who don't fit the eighteenth-century mold.

When trying to understand the damage done to children, one piece of the puzzle is the fundamental belief that education establishment is there to meet the needs of the school rather than meeting the needs of the children. This is evidenced by the current focus on the large standardized test that is returned to teachers several months after it is taken, rendering it of little value to the student's education. However, schools are judged on the test and how students reach proficiency and that is what is important to some politicians.

### Slavery Based System of Education

Let's go back in history for a better understanding of how our education system has stagnated, maintaining the status quo for the express purpose of limiting success to those who didn't fit the mold. In the late eighteenth century Thomas Jefferson described the structural design for what is now the system of education. He stated the purpose quite clearly as "Raking a few geniuses from the rubbish." Developed during slavery, in the mindset of that time, some children didn't rise to the level of rubbish and were not allowed to enter the schoolhouse door. Under that system, the "geniuses" who went to college were the sole focus while the rest were thrown out into the world to work the jobs of their parents guaranteed to never follow their dreams. Eventually slavery was abolished which meant those in power would have to find creative ways to keep a people down.

*"Our mechanical, industrialized civilization is concerned with averages, with percent's. The mental habit which reflects this social scene subordinates education and social arrangements based on averaged gross inferiorities and superiorities."* —John Dewey, 1922

That eighteenth-century system of education had many concerns, among them was that no consideration was given to the reality that students blossom at different times and in different ways. There was no need for that as those who would succeed were predetermined by race and gender. The role of those in the subclass was rarely challenged as it was ingrained in the culture of that day.

The result of the current education system leaves no doubt that the slavery based philosophy has not only continued but has flourished in today's system of education. The fundamental purpose of education continues to determine who is first and who is last in the race to nowhere. The goal remains to rake a few geniuses from the rubbish.

Dropout rates are high, letter grades and Carnegie units developed around 1900 continue to be a meaningless mainstay in the educational system and the school to prison pipeline continues to flourish. Yet agenda driven politicians continue to march on, comfortable with the same rhetoric of reform that has been successful in recent times. This group includes a wide range of those who utilize the rhetoric of the past to support an outdated system of education driven by the testing fiasco. It is in their best interest to maintain the status quo.

The current "teach to the test" curriculum combined with a devastating system of failure locks unwitting children into the subclass through the non-ending cycle of poverty. Absent quality assessments, the narrow scope of the state standardized test along with chapter tests that drive the curriculum, push children deeper into the abyss with little hope of ever feeling success.

## Confronting Poverty as a Reality

Simply put, most of those living below the Federal Poverty Level have obstacles in their way that slow their learning. With an antiquated system of failure in place, those who don't learn at the same rate and in the same way are eventually failed back to the beginning. They then become too far behind and too old to ever graduate and are subsequently pushed out of school with little hope of a well-paying job. Their children then grow up impoverished and the cycle starts all over again.

Whether it is kids living below the Federal Poverty Level in the Appalachians or in urban America, the fundamental issue is the same. Childhood stress literally slows the brain functioning while malnutrition damages the thought process, as does the lack of sleep, poor physical and mental health, and a wide range of other obstacles to learning. With those who are learning English as a second language, the problems are different. Their challenge is to learn a new language while progressing in a wide range of academic skills.

According to Dr. Kara Fitzgerald in her interview on the program "Gene Whispering" with Dr. Moshe Szyf at www.drkarafitzgerald.com on February 27, 2017 she stated, "So essentially what we saw, that a stressful environment really coordinates three kinds of responses in the body: an immune response, a metabolic response, and a behavioral response. And if you remember my talk, I talked about the fact that you can't break psychiatry from physical health. They're coordinated. When something stressful or threatening happens, it's not just our brain that is involved. We have to recruit everything from the immune system, to the fat system, to the heart. And therefore, what I believe is early in life, is children are getting this information, life is going to be tough. And they are kind of altering multiple systems to deal with hard life. And hard life involves social threat; it involves food threat, lack of food. It involves bacterial infestation, so it prepares for all of this."

As educators, we don't know whether a student is affected by these conditions or not. Therefore, we must assume they are not and assume all can reach to the stars. However, when we see a student's progress is impaired, we must recognize that there are reasons and adjust to them. Solutions are based on the need to view every child as an individual, with individual needs.

*"The biggest mistake of past centuries in teaching has been to treat all students as if they were variants of the same individual and thus to feel justified in teaching them all the same."* —Dr. Howard Gardner

There will be many contrived solutions to these social problems, but the reality is none of them will happen immediately. Fixing poverty will take decades if not centuries and the artificial educational fixes, designed in the world of make believe, will exasperate the problem. There is, however, one act that can turn education around. That one is to devise a system and philosophy of education that meets the needs of all children because all children will always be different in their learning styles, rates, and interests. With the new system, a constant flow of teacher encouragement must follow. No longer will educators see failure as evil, they will see it as part of a learning process and every step forward as a cause for celebration. Not only will that system, if done with encouragement, meet the needs of all students, it will become a major player in the process of breaking the cycle of poverty.

*Poverty is not destiny if a new system and philosophy of education is put in place to meet the needs of all.*

## OBSTACLES TO IMPROVING EDUCATION

Schools continue to search for a solution to the overlying concerns of how to move forward in the learning process, to provide the best education possible for all students. How to make the "Every Student Succeeds Act" work is the charge brought to the administration in Washington D.C. The fundamental basis of No Child Left Behind, Race to the Top, and Common Core, was and is school competition. Like with the business sector, our country was built on competition. However, there is another aspect that made our country strong and that was collaboration. Necessary to the success of a school system is that there is a good balance between the two on an even playing field.

Schools across the spectrum could have easily been innovators in education except for the greed of some, the ego of others, and the agenda driven politicians leading children into the abyss following an outmoded system of education. To some "for profit" schools, students were deemed unimportant to the profits of the school leaders. Other schools were simply developed in the way they were "supposed to," using the same outdated philosophy that has been in place for centuries. Of course, there were those who truly tried to innovate and run quality schools but how would anyone know? Due to an outdated accountability plan or no plan at all, little was known about the real quality of a school.

## THE CURSE OF SCHOOL COMPETITION

Most damaging to education in recent years was clearly competition, the race to emptiness. Competition between schools led to the effort to teach kids as objects rather than subjects. It took away the fundamental purpose of education which is to prepare children for their future and forced them into being pawns designed to enhance the perception of the school through their functioning on an artificial test.

### The Making of Wivets

In the private sector, competition is designed to make the company thrive by making a profit. In the process, they can afford to make some "less than perfect" wooden wivets if no one notices or tries to sue them. It is acceptable to cut corners if they don´t get caught. The quality of the product is secondary. Just ask Volkswagen. However, there is a significant difference between business and education. Educators can´t recall kids.

Companies can sand down the wivets to make them perfect while that object lies in one spot without thinking, acting, or reacting. They are just wivets. However, children cannot be force-fed education. You can sand a wivet to perfection if you spend more time working on it. Children open or close their minds only when they decide that the information has value to them and is presented in a way in which they can connect. Without that connection, they can sit in their seat forever and retain nothing more. Sitting time is not an issue, quality learning time is.

With competition, all schools must covet their great ideas to prove they are the best. They must be first because that is what is important. Learning will become secondary if they can echo the wills of the agenda driven politicians; then they will be adored, accepted, and ready to function in today's world. However, with competition comes more cheating, whether it was Volkswagen in the private sector or a variety of well publicized legal cases in traditional public schools as well as with charter, voucher, and private schools. With competition overriding collaboration the students are the ones that lose. The focus is now on the perceived success of the school rather than on the education of the child.

To win, administrators have become quite adept at adjusting the figures to give the perception of a quality school. The more publicized acts of deception are well known, but more subtle ways to increase the perceived quality of a school are not so visible to the naked eye. Pushing kids out of school just before the test, or by using techniques to only allow high scoring students into a school are everyday business.

*Because of competition, the goal is for your school to be first, and with any luck, other schools, along with their students will be last. The question now becomes, whose kids do we want to see fail?*

## FAILING FORWARD, WD-40 STYLE

How do we overcome the focus on school competition and shift the focus to real student needs? Now is the time to brainstorm some of the more recent attempts at reforming the education system. Although many have been horrendous failures, remember that failure is the best way to learn and improve our efforts. Without failure, nothing would be accomplished. Take the case of the lubricant, WD-40. The 40 in the name comes from the 39 failures to perfect the product with success coming on the fortieth try.

## The Process of Reform

Beginning with "Goals 2000" the standardizing of education was off to a conspicuous start expecting all children to reach competency in reading and math at the 4th, 8th, and 12th grade level. Needless to say, by the year 2000, that didn't happen. However, it began a journey down a path that was to lead to a culture of failure for students and educators alike. The good news was a strong focus on the arts was created. This focus included dance, theater, music, and the visual arts with four divisions—creation and performance; cultural and historical context; perception and analysis; and the nature and value of the arts. At the least, the arts were considered significant in the educational process.

Following Goals 2000, The No Child Left Behind Act was designed to improve on the past failures. Again, this was a devastating failure and it did damage to so many children. That bill had the false expectation that every child could be at the same place at the same time on their test-driven proficiency. In addition, the focus on the arts was nowhere to be found.

However, it was the first time that we, as a nation, started considering the importance of every child. Think about it, our education philosophy has never concerned itself with those who moved slower through the system or those who moved faster. This is a small step but an important one in the process of whole child education reform. As in WD-40, perhaps Goals 2000 would be called ER-1, NCLB should then be called ER-2, as in Educational Reform one and two.

Another formula was then attempted, ER-3. Common Core utilized a failed top down concept that subtly developed guidelines from the federal and the state level to impose on all children. Again, it was test driven thus lending itself to yet another level of failure. As test scores came in all over the board, one would wonder if they could ever succeed at getting every child to proficiency at the same time. However, the agenda driven politicians were adamant that only if given more sitting time and developing a little more grit, they would succeed. That didn't happen.

However, Common Core forced educators to look at a proficiency system of education. Letter grades and grade levels would no longer be recognized as an indicator of a student's achievement. Common Core forced educators to focus on the actual learning of each individual child. Unfortunately, they then took that information to standardize the child leading to yet another failure and the need to move on to ER-4.

A stretch of the imagination would have RTTT, The Race to The Top, as ER-4. In this race, states were awarded points for various policies that were thought to improve innovation in education. One of these was to turn around low performing schools. Of course, the failure was to base a school's success on the huge standardized test without recognizing the student's differences in those schools. They did include the Value-Added Model that used an artificial formula to seemingly give credence to some students who did not do well on the test. However, that is a far cry from taking the time and effort to follow each individual child through their progress with demonstrated learning.

With competition at is base, ER-4 forced a win lose situation on schools that drove them away from the fundamental purpose of education. Winning became more important than learning. Failing at this led to the discovery of what not to do with the system of education.

## STARTING NEW, OR MAYBE NOT

Preparations are now being made to move on to ER-5, the "Every Student Succeeds Act," with a new administration in charge at the Department of Education. Regardless of whether Common Core continues to exist, the absurdity is still with us. If replaced, the question arises; will the eighteenth-century system of education that was described by Thomas Jefferson as Raking a few geniuses from the rubbish" be again embraced? Or will there be true innovation? As the current law puts Common Core in the hands of states, it will probably be around for a while. Either way, to design a system of education for the future, these concerns must be considered:

1. Recognize that it is not the nature of human beings to be at the same place at the same time academically.
2. Build student failure into the system as a WD-40 experience, a part of the learning process.
3. Make critical thinking the primary focus of the new world system and philosophy of education.
4. Given Dr. Howard Gardner's Theory of Multiple Intelligences, allow for each child to follow their pathway to successful achievement of demonstrated proficiency.
5. Assessment, administered at the local level and monitored by the state to assure accountability, must allow for immediate feedback to teachers.
6. Assessment, no longer cheapened by the narrowed scope of a standardized test, should be broadened to become a stepping stone for the whole child learning experience.
7. School accountability must focus on a wide range of indicators including parent, student, and teacher surveys. Student achievement progress may be a consideration if done correctly.

8. Teacher accountability will mandate a wide range assessment including several classroom observations to provide support for teachers who are struggling.
9. Evaluate the relationship between competition and collaboration to assure an even balance.

These are only a few suggestions but it is a long way to ER-40. Let us hope perfection can be reached long before that. Common Core failed most, if not all guidelines necessary for a strong system of education. The time has come, not to revert to the "good old days" when education was for the privileged but to innovate forward with a system that allows all children to receive the education they deserve.

## Must Every Student Succeed the Same?

With the new administration in Washington D.C. and a new law the hope is that another step forward in the process of real education reform will be evident. Will the "Every Student Succeeds Act" really make a difference? At the least, the hope is that there will be parts of the act that allow the process of reform to continue. The reality is that some parts of the law may be helpful but others won't. Needless to say, the suggestions above are not currently within the realm of consideration. Is change in the wind or is the rhetoric of reform still the guideline. Some thoughts to consider are:

1. The testing system appears to continue the traditional focus with the exception that some states can apply to try out innovative assessments. The "Every Student Succeeds Act" (ESSA), through a provision presented by Senators Susan Collins and Bernie Sanders, allows a limited number of schools to provide innovative assessments in lieu of the test.
2. There does not seem to be an effort to change the antiquated failure system in schools. However, there is no rule that mandates that system of failure.
3. As the standardized test remains the norm, creative thinking will remain at a minimum. However, for those states that develop local assessments in accordance with the ESSA, the possibility exists to use demonstrations of learning or project based assessment to allow creative thinking to be part of the process.
4. Whether driven by the test or even a more acceptable assessment, the student's individual pathway to success would remain non-existent.
5. There seems to be little evidence that test information will be returned to teachers within an acceptable time frame, thus rendering it useless.
6. Most tests will maintain the narrow scope of past years. However, this could change with the states who will be allowed to innovate.

7. Although school success indicators focus on proficiency on an artificial test, the door is left open for parent, student, and teacher surveys as well as additional indicators to be included.
8. Teacher assessments are no longer required to use test scores as an indicator of teacher quality. This leaves the states struggling to figure out what to do next.
9. Clearly competition is still the mainstay and the driving force behind school and student failure. There are no signs of this changing.

The one saving grace is that teachers still control the classroom.

## ADVOCATING FOR CHANGE: JUST THE FACTS

### Justifying Change

Moving forward, advocates for the agenda of children must stand together to make a clear statement. Our current system of education is broken and well-certified teachers know how to fix it. Preparing for ER-6 and beyond is a difficult task and to accomplish this, educators must all be on the same page.

Those supporting the public sector spew out all the problems with the current testing fiasco. However, their concern for the quality of the test often fades when the scores show in their favor. It is difficult to avoid this problem because there are no accurate assessment processes available for comparison. However, if the politicians would kindly step aside, quality certified teachers will build that process beginning with the knowledge that the "test" is a lousy indicator of achievement!

Given that there are millions of students in the school system with a range of skills and abilities from the severest of the cognitive disabled children across the board to those "book learned" students who are good test takers, why would anyone ever think every child would be in the same place on a standardized test on the same day the test is given? It is not human nature for all children to be the same. Do they get their teeth at the same time, start talking at the same time, start walking at the same time or recognize colors at the same time? Then why would we demand they learn a wide variety of educational skills at the same time?

More important is the misconception that children demonstrate learning solely with paper and pencil in hand. The limited scope of the artificial test uses a completely different mindset than does the real quest for knowledge. A true demonstration of learning allows the student to utilize critical thinking as well as a wide variety of "whole child" skills to resolve a problem. When we then recognize learning is personal, connecting to a student's background knowledge enhances the probability of success and provides a stepping stone to unfamiliar territory. Critical thinking, essential to everyday life, must be a mainstay of every system of education.

The system must be fixed to get rid of false indicators of academic achievement, no matter who the scores favor. Teachers of kindred mind must stay on message acknowledging that a higher level "whole child" learning is the ultimate goal.

> *"when achievement is restricted to grades, (test scores) attendance, and behavioral compliance, the robust nature of learning is inadvertently restricted . . . traditional school outcomes as level B achievement can occur in the absence of learning how to work and learn independently; (A level learning includes) learning how to synthesize, transfer and apply knowledge to the world beyond the classroom; learning how to value self as subjects and not as objects; and learning how to engage in and share power in democratic spaces."* —Dr. Angela Dye

Is that not what we want for our children, a first-class education? That's the message that must go out. It is not sufficient to simply say the test is bad. Explain why the test is bad and how it can be replaced.

There are many band-aid style approaches to resolving the problems inherent in education that are suggested by those who seek simple answers to complex questions. But it all begins with abolishing a singular indicator of success or failure. That means not only getting rid of the grandiose test, but that also goes for chapter tests that simply require the right answer. As a unit, educators along with parent's must stand together, unwavering, to replace the standardized test with true assessment, not to make it easier for teachers but to make it more effective for students.

## The Agenda of Children

When supporting the agenda of children, the whole truth will eventually surface. Achieving that whole truth requires the guidance of the best teachers, those who are fully educated, well experienced, and have an in-depth knowledge of their students and how they learn. This is accomplished by taking the handcuffs off those well experienced teachers who serve the students who need us the most. Placing those teachers in the forefront of a new whole child reform movement will require a unity of thought focusing on specific systemic changes that will enhance the education of every child. It is not enough to say what is wrong with education, innovative solutions must be offered.

Perceptions are real to those who have them. Marching and protesting the closing of schools is extremely important to provide awareness but care must be taken to avoid the perception of a self-serving agenda. We must always put the agenda of children in the forefront of our actions. The system of education is broken but it has been broken for a long time. The message that must go out is that only strong qualified teachers have the innovative skills to fix it. Those teachers truly understand the only way forward is to challenge the ways of the past with creative, innovative ideas that truly respect the intelligence and abilities of all children. That is the message that will resonate and that message must be shouted from the roof-tops, in a singular voice.

## Think While it is Still Legal

Evaluating the current system and philosophy of education, it is difficult to find a strong emphasis on critical thinking. There is an effort to assure students give the right answers to the right questions, but little effort to turn students loose to research and challenge ideas. This would require answers that might not agree with the teacher, the text-book, or the standardized test, but of significance is that the students would be able to stretch their minds to the heavens and beyond. This is pretty scary to the politicians because it takes away their power.

If they wanted children to learn to think critically, they would have done it long ago. Comedian George Carlin makes this point: *"They don't want a population of citizens capable of critical thinking. They don't want well-informed, well-educated people capable of critical thinking. They're not interested in that! That doesn't help them. That's against their interests. You know something? They don't want people who are smart enough to sit around the kitchen table and figure (things) out. . . . They want obedient workers"*! That is the fundamental purpose of education today. To toe the line! What does thinking have to do with it? It is time to bolster thinking while it is still legal.

Children learn more and learn faster when they are empowered to explore and discover their own answers rather than simply regurgitating someone else's information, quickly memorized and soon forgotten. What do you, the reader remember looking back on your educational experience?

To control thinking in schools, some states have their Board of Education frantically spending hours trying to determine which historical heroes would be allowed to grace the pages of their text books for their children to idolize. A simple solution would be to empower students to discover and justify their own heroes. In years gone by, this would take weeks in a library. Today the information is at their fingertips. No longer must students drudge through encyclopedias and countless library books to collect data when they can get the same information with a search engine in five minutes.

What if children questioned who really discovered America? Would the answer be Columbus or would it be Native Americans or Asians coming through the Bering Strait area? The Vikings, under Leif Erickson were in

Canada 500 years before Columbus made his trip. Did Columbus ever make it to North America? Let students discover the answers.

What if students were asked who was the first to actually stand on the North Pole? As it appears, Robert Perry's expedition could have been the first however many say Frederick Cook came sooner. Others say Perry lagged behind on the actual day someone stood on the North Pole to allow Matthew Henson or the Inuit Indians to be the first. Let the students discover it for themselves. Who was the first to fly an airplane? Was it the Wright Brothers or Gustave Whitehead? And slavery did exist, and the slaves brought an amazing number of skills with them. What were these skills? These questions go on forever. Just imagine how much children can learn when they are allowed to explore and use critical thinking?

Competition and collaboration have been a part of the culture of our country for many years. The secret is to keep a good balance between them. Envision a school system where collaboration is the primary goal, and critical thinking leads to the student's conclusions. Envision a world of education where charters, choice, private, and traditional public schools worked together in the best interest of children. Envision a system that didn't put students in the middle of a battle to determine who wins and who loses, where performance on a test didn't define who they are and all schools served the children who need us the most.

*When the system of education changes from competition to collaboration, the world of education turns upside down and children become the winners.*

School systems, by design, are a well-structured cast system designed to educate the few while ignoring those ordinary students who don't fit into the contrived parameters of what they call success. Those quality teachers who attempt to circumvent this system are systematically drawn back by the powers of the new status quo into an educational world that quashes their talents.

Now it is well past time for those teachers to take on the challenge of changing education for the better. Never in our country's history has it been so important for education professionals to stand up and be heard to assure a free and appropriate education for every child. Educators are poised and ready for change. The kind of change that allows them to teach in the way children learn best and for children to learn in that manner. Educators are ready for the kind of change that resolves the age-old problem of truancy, school dropouts, failed students, unequal student treatment, low or no levels of learning, and many more.

Teachers are ready for the kind of change that brings out the genius in every child. They are ready for the kind of change that assures learning for all and where "no child left behind" is not just a slogan. Educators stand on the brink of providing the kind of change that raises this country up to new heights, with future leaders of the twenty-first century in the forefront. Teachers have been prepared to encourage critical, rational thinking from their students if only allowed to do so. This will not be given to teachers, it must be taken. There is no time to ask permission, the time is now for teachers to step up and take action!

This kind of change isn't easy and many won't understand it. But if educators truly want to serve all children, the effort will be worthwhile. No longer may teachers look into the eyes of students the system has failed and see hopelessness. The time is now to develop a system and philosophy of education that recognizes the whole child. The time is now to bring back hope to every child.

The time has come to forge forward into the future of education with the clear purpose of serving all students by guiding them toward their individual future. Reconstructing the educational design of schools is essential to the change that is needed. The fundamental purpose of a school under the new design is to not give up on any child; but to guide each child from an individual beginning to completion no matter how long it takes.

The effort must now be made to seek positive solutions to achieve whole child reform that truly serves all children and even some adults. It is time to develop schools that allow teachers to teach and students to learn. An incentive to develop such a school is the freedom for educators to take back their profession and children to embrace the joy of learning once again. Erase from your mind how schools are supposed to be and think about how schools can be to serve all children, rising above the confirmation bias to embrace critical thinking necessary for everyday life.

*"We are still trying to develop both the philosophy as well as a system of education which really does respect the intelligence and abilities of ordinary people."* —James Anderson

*Chapter 2*

# Don't Believe Anything You See or Hear

Going through life without critical thinking is like living in a dream, and then you wake up. Your fantasy world disappears and real-life smacks you in the face. But you are saved, you can go right back to sleep, and all is well. Critical and rational thinking might not give you the solutions you want, but they provide a reality that is so important in many aspects of everyday life.

Simple solutions to complex problems may satisfy your need to be right, but critical, rational thinking will lead to the truth and that is far better in the long run. The challenge to educators is to shift the emphasis from the result to the process, to bring George Carlin's "kitchen table" into the classroom and take the students out to that "kitchen table" called the community to allow them to explore and think beyond that small box full of word games and math riddles.

Teachers must break-out of the shackles that hold them to an antiquated system of education. No longer may they succumb to the wishes of the politicians, forced to manipulate students into compliance.

It is the role of the innovative teacher to open the minds of all students to a new way of thinking, their own. Teachers truly understand education and their voice is essential to the development of a new world system of education.

The current, outmoded system of education has diminished if not eliminated critical thinking. This is accomplished by forcing simple answers to complex questions to narrow the scope of the young minds they are there to teach. When did you ever see a question on a standardized test that ended with the phrase "I could be wrong?" That is not likely because the test is always right. Children are taught to believe what they are told in the classroom thus leading into a mindset where they believe everything they hear. "It must be right, it's on Facebook."

## THE CHILDS RIGHT TO THINK

What can education do to support a child's right to think? There are many pieces to the education puzzle but in the lead, is critical and rational thinking supported by research, research, and more research. This is so much easier today. In years gone by, hours and hours not to mention days, weeks and months were needed to come up with information that can now be found on the internet in minutes. But not so fast, remember no one knows if those internet sources are accurate.

John Merrow as written in his blog The Merrow Report; Educators must Step Up: "Today's young people need guidance in learning how to sift through the flood of information (much of it fake news) and turn it into knowledge." There is a ton of information out there on the internet, but what is real and what is not? Don't believe anything you see or hear. Question everything until you come up with a satisfactory solution.

Advertising is a good example. Whether it is in politics or for our favorite beverage it is flashed on our television screens, across our computers, on billboards, on the radio, in newspapers, in magazines, and everywhere we look. How much of that is the whole truth and how much is deception. Is a huge truck stronger because the man in the commercial has a deep voice? Will everyone look ten years younger if they buy that anti-aging cream?

So, reach into your pocket or better yet, grab your credit card and buy that truck because that is what a real man will do and purchase that serum; at least it's cheaper than plastic surgery. People are manipulated on a regular basis and it is time to educate our children out of this mess while bolstering their right to think.

When talking about digging into our pocket, be prepared to dig deep. Jonah Berger is a professor at the Wharton School of the University of Pennsylvania On season 5 episode 4 of National Geographics "Brain Games," Berger states: "Seeing a higher price tag often makes us believe that product is simply better." Berger continues, "your brain has a complicated recipe for assigning pleasure to value." Without going into details, the bottom line is your brain tells you a higher price means higher quality. That's the way the brain works. But it is not as simple as it seems. Once the brain accepts that concept, it looks to background knowledge to adapt its thoughts. That's where education can play a role if it uses critical and rational thinking as a basis for decision making.

## CRITICAL THINKING IN EVERYDAY LIFE

Educating children is a difficult job. While some subjects are deemed important to politicians, others seem to have lost value. As the transition is made to critical thinking, a strong focus must be placed on what is necessary in everyday life. After all, the fundamental purpose of education is to prepare students for life in their future. Here we look at some areas of study that may no longer exist within some school curricula and how they relate to critical thinking necessary for success.

Significant is to keep a focus on the subject matter discussed in each of these areas. It is not necessary to include these areas of interest as classes, isolated by their subject matter. What is important is to bring back the content described as part of an integrated curriculum, building a wide range of skills necessary for a successful life for every child.

In today's new world of education, quality teachers have the ability to teach across curriculum to integrate a wide variety of subject matter with the fundamentals of reading, and math so essential to every student's future. What better way to teach reading than incorporate it into a home economics project where students do the research, develop a plan of action, make a presentation, and write a final synopsis. Reading, writing, speaking, and critical thinking are essential to a child's future. When students read in the context of something that is real to them, they will develop much faster than when those readings are isolated into a contrived setting.

## Managing the Economy of the Home

Is it important to understand the simple task of taking care of the economy in the home? The answer to that question is a resounding YES! A well-organized household budget would increase the quality of life for each person involved. So many people today are either incapable of doing a budget, or simply don't find it important enough. The effect may be much greater than is believed. That is why it must be taught.

Consider this, there are two years in history where household debt becomes 100 percent of the gross domestic product, 1929 and 2007 according to Columbia professor David Beam. The result in both cases was a depression and near depression. This was a disaster waiting to happen. Not only is the quality of life diminished without a strong household budget, the entire country is affected.

This information led Professor Beam to say, "The problem is us. It is not the banks, greedy though they may be, overpaid though they may be. The problem is us . . . we've been living high on the hog. Our living standard has been rising dramatically in the last 25 years. And we have been borrowing much of the money to make that prosperity happen."

Let's go shopping to see how rational thinking can help us bring our household budget under control. When purchasing an antihistamine is the brand name better than the store brand? The brand name may be highly respected, but it costs more. But, wait a minute, look at the ingredients. They appear to be identical. It's up to the consumer to determine which product to purchase but the key is research and critical thinking. Are there differences in the production of the product that would make the consumer choose one over the other or are they really the same?

The bottom line is to stay within a household budget and put the credit cards away by using common sense and comparative shopping. This may seem like common sense to most of us but, preparing students with this knowledge and how to fit it into a budget is essential for a quality of life.

Students must be encouraged to use their brain in many ways. Look at the product on the shelf. Look at the per unit price comparison. Look at the ingredients, and after doing that, test the product in your daily life. But remember, your brain will tell you the most expensive item is best. Don't ever believe what your brain tells you until you fully research the data. Don't let your brain lie to you.

## Is it Really Just Shop Class?

Critical thinking is essential to everyday life. What if you need a new kitchen cabinet to hold all your "stuff?" As we know, the more stuff we get, the more room we need to store it. In a store a simple kitchen cabinet can cost a significant amount of money. Do you go without the cabinet because it doesn't fit into your budget, or do you get creative?

It is phenomenal what you can do with a hammer, some nails, wood, a tape measure, and a level. Simply go on a search engine or Youtube.com where complete instructions are available. You might want to know how to use the tools, the safety precautions needed, and the critical thinking necessary to make the cabinet to precise measurements. That is not difficult if you know how.

As a child, this author along with friends Mike Heckathorn and Bob O'Leary built a shack with those simple supplies. We drew plans, located the wood from a junk pile behind our garage, measured each board, and cut them to size. There was a lot of trial and error but that's how we learn. We don't learn by getting it right, we learn by getting it wrong and making adjustments where needed. If it can be done at age 10, anyone can do it and with Home Maintenance and Repair class, (or math class) it will be a cinch. These skills must be incorporated into the curriculum.

To teach the whole child, we can no longer simply prepare students solely for jobs. We may not continue with the absurd belief that no one needs to repair their cars, fix their homes, or manage a budget to purchase items that are best fitted for the needs of the household. Who hasn't driven through an urban community to observe someone fixing their own car? Most people drive a car, shouldn't most people understand how to check the oil or change the oil or do simple car maintenance? Don't be fooled into believing you have to spend a lot of money for every household item. Don't automatically believe the advertising. Think and research and you might find a better way.

## RE-Inventing the Math Curriculum

Critical thinking is the corner stone of a student's future both on the job and in daily life. It is important to prioritize subject matter that demands the kind of thinking that leads to real-life decisions. Begin by looking at the outdated mathematics curriculum. Yes, math is factual in its event. We must, however, explore what elements of math are to be taught and to whom. It is time to take a good hard look at the math curriculum.

Which comes first, algebra or geometry? In the traditional, yet irrational, step-by-step process of education, algebra has historically been a pre-requisite to geometry. That seems logical because many believe geometry is more difficult or requires the skills learned in algebra to succeed. But is it rational?

That process does not take into consideration how the brain works. Dr. Temple Grandon talks about the differences in brains. She says that she has the type of brain that sees things in pictures. She was horrible at algebra and thus was not allowed to take trigonometry or geometry in school. However, she discovered that she was superb at trigonometry and geometry and went on to become famous designing cattle shoots throughout the country using those skills.

The reality is different brains see things differently. Human beings are not all extensions of the same person. No longer may educators demand that everyone thinks alike forcing those like Dr. Grandon to do well on subjects in which they are less skilled before taking the subjects in which they excel. That is not rational.

Due to the long history of artificial education, Dr. Grandon had trouble with algebra and might have failed many subjects if it were not for a loving family and support, especially from her science teacher who provided a wide range of "hands on" projects for her. Although autistic and a genius, she was seen as a failure simply because she had a different brain.

Dr. Grandon knows the differences in brains and acknowledges the need for all different types of brains in our world. That's why educators must reconsider the one size fits all approach to the mathematics curriculum. After all, there is no rationale that would indicate whether algebra or geometry is more important to any one student. The question becomes, what fits into the individual student's real-life needs.

Where does statistics fit into the picture? Consider that basic inferential statistics might be more useful to the average person than algebra or geometry.

Although inferential statistics sounds difficult, it is no more of a challenge to students than any of the other areas of mathematics. Consider the impact it has on our understanding of the irrational world we live in. We see on the never-ending news cycle that a Mexican undocumented immigrant was charged with a violent crime. The media repeats it over and over again and politicians see an opportunity to comment on one side or the other.

And then the viewing public is reminded of ten or twelve other examples of those who have committed crimes with the expectation that the information be generalized into an entire population. Remember how the brain works especially when irrational fears are added. If twelve Mexican undocumented immigrants out of the 11,000,000 in this country committed a serious crime, does that mean the other 10,999,988 are criminals? That's what our brain will believe if allowed to.

In the name of critical thinking, the reader is encouraged to determine the statistics through their own research. Fear locks in our beliefs and the lack of knowledge of statistics adds to the confusion. It is time to focus on math that can be useful in daily life and inferential statistics leads the list.

Once fear takes hold, it is nearly impossible for one to talk their brain out of that fault. The solution, however, is critical and rational thinking. The statistics will give students a better idea of whether they should succumb to fear or simply ignore another political deception. Don't believe anything you see or hear . . . Study it research it and search for the truth. Do the math, do the research and only when you, the student is satisfied with the findings, believe the data. In education, teachers must turn students loose with guidance to determine their own conclusions. And then discuss the results. Critical and rational thinking is the solution. After all, what is the fundamental purpose of education anyway? To win or to learn how to thrive in one's own community?

*The nature of those trying to impose a political agenda on you, is to strike fear into your daily thought processes. Don't be conned!*

## Civics, How Does Government Work

It is not in the interest of politicians that children, not to mention adults, develop an understanding of how the government operates. That way they can promise the sun, the stars and the moon, and the voting public would be none the wiser. Of course, the politician will put a chicken in every pot and a car in every garage. And taxes will come down and income will rise, and all will be well with the world. Don't believe it!

There are a few issues missing in those promises that students must understand. Of most significance is how they are going to accomplish those goals.

A presidential candidate can promise everything to the voter but can accomplish nothing if what was promised was illegal according to the constitution or undesirable to the majority in Congress. Everything must begin with Congress. Without a bill from Congress, there would be no bill for the president to sign. And if the courts determine the promise to be illegal, it is dead in the water before it begins.

We must teach children there are three equal divisions of government that must be in synch for any bill to succeed. And a chicken in every pot and a car in every garage isn't even a bill. The legislative branch, the executive branch, and the judicial branch must all be in synch for any promise to be kept.

*The Supreme court interprets the constitution, not politicians, or any other group. Students must study the constitution, and, in doing so, must look at the Supreme Court decisions that are relevant. These court decisions must be examined to help students fully understand our government.*

The problem, however, is that few people seem to know how government functions. That's where a community-based school can thrive. Students must study the fundamentals of government to assure they have a clear understanding of the political process. They then visit the different branches of government in their area or their state capital or even in Washington D.C. and ask questions upon questions, like, how are you going to put a chicken in every pot? How are you going to get lower taxes through Congress and what are the consequences of lowering taxes on the overall budget, or the overall economy. An entire unit in school could be devoted to devising questions to ask your local politicians utilizing critical thinking.

Just think of a political campaign in light of the need for critical thinking. Deception is everyday business as every candidate tries to convince the voter they are the one to best serve their constituents needs. But why don't candidates tell the truth? Why is deception necessary? New Jersey Governor Chris Christie said that if you don't want politicians to lie, don't expect them to align perfectly to your beliefs. Children must use critical thinking to prioritize the issues that are important to them and then determine whether those issues are legal and can make it through Congress. Then they will determine if the candidate has the skills to get that issue through Congress.

If politicians are expected to agree with everything every human being in this country wants, there will soon be a rude awakening. Politicians then must lie. They must say one thing to one audience and another to a different group. Thus, the liar in chief will convince everyone that he or she is on their side on every issue when that is impossible. Students must be allowed to utilize deep, rational thinking to truly make wise decisions. That process must begin in school.

The role of education is not to take one side or another in a political debate. It is to create an environment conducive to rational, critical thinking with the hope that students will internalize that and carry it with them throughout life. And they must learn to go out of their comfort zone for the sake of truth.

Of utmost importance is to encourage students to get involved in the process. There is no better way to understand the political process than to get in the middle of it. They can get involved in non-partisan projects as part of their Social Studies class. Have them run a conference on an issue that benefits the community as a class project. Or they can connect with their favorite politician. The bottom line is to get involved now.

Many academics can be built into every project on the individual's level of achievement. This is to get the juices flowing. Students then must be encouraged to become involved in the politics of their choice outside the school. Embrace the politics they believe in and learn first-hand as they grow. There is no better way to understand the world than to dive into the middle of it.

## IT'S THE BRAIN STUPID!

As students grow they must be alert to the reality that they will be conned in every way possible throughout life. Wise decisions are essential to survival and to make wise decisions one must look carefully at every opportunity that comes before them. Do not believe anything you hear and half of what you see. Question everything put before you, assume nothing is at it seems.

The lack of critical thinking allows people to have a narrow view of the world around them. There is a case where a politician picked up a snowball from outside and brought it in to the capital to demonstrate why global warming is a hoax. This example leads us to the need to integrate science and math with reading and research to understand today's serious issues.

To understand global warming for example, we must first realize what global means. That should give a hint as to the intensity of the problem. The globe, or the world, is huge. To be more accurate, it is said to be 24,901.45053 miles around. And the Earth's surface is estimated at 196,900,000 square miles.

According to Livescience.com, "Global warming is the term used to describe a gradual increase in the average temperature of the Earth's atmosphere and its oceans, a change that is believed to be permanently changing the Earth's climate." Putting the emphasis on the words "average temperature" makes clear the enormity of the problem. Can this be determined by picking up a snowball from one square foot of land?

Don't believe anything you see or hear. If children are taught to question everything, they will be forced to think critically. Instead, children are often taught to obey and accept without question. In school, they must believe and respond to the right answers for the chapter or standardized test or they will FAIL!

There are many issues on all sides of the spectrum that are of concern. It is important not to generalize issues, but to look at them in detail as specifics. The constant generalization of issues forces irrational, simplistic responses. When someone gives you a generalized response to a question, ask them to be specific, and watch them squirm.

The reality is, no matter how much evidence is presented, many still believe the snowball theory. Why don't people believe in science that is based on facts instead of believing some outrageous unproven theory that makes no sense what so ever? It is simple to blame those who seem to have irrational ideas stuck in their minds, but there is much more to it. Looking deeper into the problem we come across the "Bayesian Confirmation Bias." This theory is defined as the tendency to interpret new evidence as confirmation of ones existing beliefs or theories.

## RISING ABOVE THE CONFIRMATION BIAS

Once you establish a certain belief you tend to favor that belief, although that belief is not absolute in nature. According to Science Daily, "Confirmation bias is a phenomenon wherein decision makers have been shown to actively seek out and assign more weight to evidence that confirms their hypothesis and ignore or under weigh evidence that could disconfirm their hypothesis." This happens especially when that belief provides a comforting conclusion to an emotionally charged experience, it then becomes locked into one's thoughts.

We often believe what we want to believe based on the "confirmation bias." But what is the solution? Teachers could throw up their hands and let students believe what they want no matter how irrational, or they can take action. Here are comments from University of Virginia Psychologist Dr. Jim Coan on the Netflix series "Brain Games": "When you hear an idea or a statement your pre-frontal cortex helps you decide if it's true or false. . . . In order for your brain to make sense of a new idea, it will initially believe it, but then your brain immediately begins to check the idea against your memory to see if it fits with everything else you know to be true. For a moment, your brain will believe almost everything it hears."

The broader the student's background knowledge, the better chance they will seek out a more rational answer. Put science out in the forefront and let them dig into it. Then when they take that second look and check the initial idea against their memory, they will have a basis of fact to work from. Ingrain deep thinking as a way of life and they will continue the process of critical thinking on a daily basis. When you repeat to your students "Don't believe anything you hear and half of what you see," you will remind them to take a deeper look at all the evidence before reaching a conclusion.

*The greatest challenge to educators in this decade is to prepare children to rise above the confirmation bias and embrace critical thinking.*

When a student is involved in a project that relates to the subject at hand, their thinking goes far deeper than simply stating the first step of the scientific method. The student develops a hypothesis, tests it, retests it, refines, or rejects it, fails and moves forward until that student achieves success.

## OPENING THE DOORS TO CRITICAL THOUGHT

### Thinking beyond Failure

Currently failure has a negative effect on children that might well be the main reason for the high dropout rate. It is based on a narrow scope of learning and the ever-present time frames. Add to that the lack of a process for children to overcome failure and a disaster is at hand.

How often would you accept that failing mark on your paper or be told, "You failed again." How often can educators tell students "you must repeat that grade or that subject, from the beginning?" Before too long the message will be believed, you do not belong here. When a child becomes demoralized, categorized, shamed, depressed, and thus does not belong, failure becomes a self-fulfilling prophecy.

Remember the frontal lobe? One has the tendency to believe what one is told. And if they are told they are failures long enough, that is what takes hold. "They said I could not do it, therefore I can't do it." The children then go where they are accepted, and often that isn't a good place.

Look at your own life and all the little failures you had on your job. As people learn from their failures they recover and move on. Under the current system, when students fail, they have a very limited chance to recover and move on. Those who lack a strong support system have almost no chance to succeed. The failure system in school is so entrenched that educators don't seem to notice the damage they are doing to students. Always believe failure is a stepping-stone to success and you will never again believe you, as a student, are a failure.

To achieve beyond failure, critical thinking is essential. Once a child believes failure is their next best teacher, it then becomes an essential chapter of their success story. Every "failure" gets analyzed scrutinized and dissected until the cause of that failure is determined and the door opens to the next step in the process. This takes an extraordinary effort by the student and a teacher who truly believes in an education process that not only allows but also expects a student to think.

Never again will that teacher give a failing grade. In fact, never again will that teacher give any letter grade designed to simplify a complex process. That is why education is so important to the future not only of individual citizens but of our country. Students must dig deep and seek out the true facts in a timely fashion before the irrational world swallows them up. Assessment must then tell students what they have learned as well as specify failures so that can become a tool of success.

## Don't Ever Believe You Are a Failure

If children believe everything they hear, they will believe they are less of an asset to their community if they don't go to a university. If you go to any secondary school and ask them if they are going to college, the answer will be a resounding yes! If you ask what they want to do for a living, you will get everything from a brain surgeon to a "I don't know" depending on how well they are prepped.

Students must do better than going through the motions of simply raising their hands when asked if they want to go to college. They must have a plan to determine what they want for a future, and then devise multiple possible pathways to achieve their goals.

*Every child must believe they are capable of achieving the highest level of employment possible, especially those jobs that require a college education. Then they can make a rational decision about their future.*

It is essential that students be empowered to seek their passion. Tiger Moms or over-zealous educators must never take that power away from the students. Making college a goal for students without any concept of what they want for their future is like getting on a plane without knowing its destination. Of course, we want to prepare students for success in whatever direction they go. Currently, post-secondary education of some sort is almost essential.

Educators must encourage all children to believe in their abilities to achieve whatever they desire and introduce them to as many professions as possible, especially those requiring a post-secondary education. However, they must empower students to make their own decisions based on those desires and critical thinking.

Never should we blame and shame those who do not choose higher education. No longer may students be ashamed of being plumbers, electricians, service men and women, entrepreneurs, construction workers, and others who aren't afraid to get their hands dirty. All students must be assured that if they want a university education, it is there for them and with hard work, a good focus, and critical thinking, they will succeed.

Here is a story about Willie. Willie was one of the highest performing students in middle school. His reading level was at twelfth grade level. When it came time to make a career choice, he chose not to go to college. Should he feel ashamed that he didn't take that direction? Should he feel ashamed that, instead, he chose to join the US Army and serve in Korea? And when he returned, he took a job as a welder. Not only is he doing what he loves, he is also paid well. If you get a chance, ask him how he is doing on his college loan.

*All students must have confidence that they can pursue any job they desire. However, we must remember, it is their life and their decision.*

## Question Everything

How do we make the transition from a system of education that tells children what they must know, to one that empowers them to explore and utilize critical and rational thinking? It is clear that we may not remain on the same path, the same failed system, and philosophy of education that had controlled children for centuries. Children, as they become adults, may no longer continue to wait to be told what to think and then follow like lemmings to the sea only to end up controlled by the politicians.

The first step is for children to simply not believe anything they see or hear. It is important for them to question everything and immediately because once a thought settles in, the brain holds on to it with all its might. The days of the standardized test, or even the chapter test driving the curriculum must come to an end. The days of having students regurgitate the answers that are given them just to get a letter grade are over. Let them explore and discover ideas.

Put the choices to the students and let them figure it out. What about a paper or a speech on the subject by all students presented to the rest of the class? Have a debate on the subject? Have students back their information with facts or beliefs they choose. Educators must become coaches as much as they are teachers and lead by questioning students more than answering their questions.

Let students explore and come up with their own beliefs. Allow others to question their decisions but always respect their thoughts. The information on all sides is presented and that is a good thing. The job of the teacher is to focus on the validity of the process, and then question students encouraging them to justify their conclusions.

## Finding the Pathway to Critical Thought

To devise a pathway to open the doors for critical thought for every child, first recognize that children are not the same and that learning is complex and individual. Every child has a different brain and every child comes from their own individual culture. Not just the culture of ethnicity, although that is part of the puzzle, the individual culture in which they live every day is significant to their success. Be mindful that as a new system and philosophy is being developed, it is critical for the reader to understand specifically how students learn and progress through this system.

Educating our youth is a complex issue requiring the best teachers to pull out all their resources to teach every child as a unique individual. Highly qualified teachers who fully understand human growth and development, who understand the need for individualization and are willing to put in hours of planning for every lesson are those who will lead the way to "reforming" the artificial reform movement. They are the ones who will take back their profession from those who simply teach to the test and toe the line with the textbook companies to make all children identical.

To assure a pathway to success, the system and philosophy of the traditional school must change. No longer may the antiquated model, designed over two hundred years ago, be followed. This new system must be created to allow teachers to teach according to high teaching standards, and students to learn in the way they learn best to achieve their highest standards. When children are told what their future should look like, they should simply not believe anything they hear. They should discover their future.

## What Can Parents Do to Promote Critical Thinking?

It is incumbent upon parents to team with educators to become full partners in the educational process of their children. The parent can then support the concept of critical thinking as well as encourage it daily at home. To make this effective, teachers must provide parents with ongoing information about daily lessons as well as providing home projects that encourage deep thought. The age-old practice of completing mindless homework will then be replaced by activities designed to stretch the minds of the child in conjunction with family members. A project may include an interview at a local business and could well look like this:

Dear parent:
   Please complete one of the following activities with your son/daughter: (please put a check mark by your choice)

A. ___We acted out the role-play situation of my child doing an educational survey.

B. ___ I observed my son/daughter presenting a survey to a businessperson. Here is the script:

I am a student from Midtown Middle School and I am asking questions to business people designed to provide a better education for students. Would you have a few minutes to answer some questions?

What is the most important attribute you look for in hiring a new employee?

How important is prior experience when you consider hiring a new employee?

When hiring someone straight out of school, how important is grade point average?

How much consideration is giving to the appearance of the prospective employee?

Thank you for your cooperation

Sincerely,

This project not only gives the student an understanding of the purpose of a survey, it also leaves the student with information important to their future job search. The parent becomes the teacher and is fully involved in the process encouraging their child to think deeply about the importance of a job interview.

This project encourages parents to buy into the need for daily critical thinking. An actual interview with an employer can strip away the myths of what employers are looking for and provide the reality. This result may surprise many but that is why critical thinking is so important in everyday life.

Encouraging parents to understand the role of critical thinking is necessary for every educator. A secondary goal is to develop a group of parents who will advocate for systemic change. Once this group is formed, parents become the driving force in improving and reforming education for all children. One issue most likely to unify parents is that of the antiquated standardized test. It is important for parents to fully understand the impact of this test on the diminishing role of critical thinking.

Students shudder when they realize it is time to take that all-important standardized test. On the day before the test, an announcement comes through the public-address system "Remember to get enough sleep tonight and eat a good breakfast. Tomorrow you will be taking the huge test and your school is counting on you." If that doesn't strike fear into a third grader, nothing will. Trembling, the child goes home to pass that information on to their parents. Going to bed early, the child tosses and turns and somehow makes it through the night without a lick of sleep. Following a good breakfast that sits somewhere near the top of their stomach the entire day, they nervously march on to school.

Nowhere near prepared to take the test, those young children somehow make it through the day. At least most of them do. If they have special needs and their reading is not at the proficient level, they may leave the test crying or feel the need to vomit but that's alright according to the agenda driven politicians. After all, if they believe everything they hear, they would accept themselves as failures. Children, don't believe everything you see or hear. You have your own genius. Your charge, if you accept, is to search for it, find it, and live it!

Now let's take a large dose of reality. One portion of the announcement was accurate. A good score will help the school but how will it improve critical thinking? It is always good to have loyalty to a school but to what degree? When it causes you to cry, get sick, or have a completely miserable day, it is not alright.

Now comes another reality. The test results don't get back to the teacher for several months rendering them completely useless. Assessment is only as good as the information gathered and its application to the education of the child. Four months later not only is the child at a different skill level, but the teacher has already prepared the student's educational plan.

Dr. Nicki Woodsen, a superintendent in an Indiana Public School told her teachers to do their own assessment to prepare their plans in a timely manner. As she explained that to her school systems Board of Education, they understood and agreed. It is essential for any assessment information to be in the hands of the teacher immediately. Absent that, the test is rendered useless for students. Therefore, the pressure of the test constitutes a scam of unprecedented levels. Parents and students alike are lied to for the sake of a school's proficiency rating. They are told the test is for the students.

Critical thinking does not relate to simply giving a correct answer on a test. True critical thinking is a process that rarely is accomplished in an hour or even a day. Assessing students requires an ongoing process that takes time and effort. It takes digging deep into how students are following that process and how they are arriving at their solutions. That cannot be accomplished solely with pencil and paper in hand.

The time is upon us to support teachers who refused to follow along like the proverbial lemmings to allow the test to drive the curriculum. Teaching to the test forces unsuspecting students to spend much or their educational lives preparing for something other than their real future needs. Not only is it a horrendous waste of time, it takes them away from a whole child education that truly meets the fundamental purpose of education, preparing them for their future in their community.

Teachers must awaken and take a stand. Either you are a part of the problem or a part of the solution. Don't allow the politicians to continue to deceive the public with educational double talk. Get some guts, let your voice be heard.

> *Parents; next time there is a huge test, don't believe anything you hear and half of what you see. If your child doesn't take that test, nothing will be missed. The test is for the school, not for the children. Protect your child from the influence of politicians.* ***OPT OUT!***

## Chapter 3

# Sneaking and Conniving

For any plan to succeed, as educators we must maintain our focus. It is easy to get distracted by the deceptive tactics used by some politicians to give the appearance of a successful school. Regardless of the fake success stories that abound, we must continue to work toward the goal of true whole child reform.

The naysayers will be relentless. They will question your test scores and brag about how their artificial success is somehow real. Truth be told, many schools work hard to deceive the public and will challenge you to do the same. While others sneak and connive, educators must remain straight forward and honest. They must not fall into the trap of dependence on test scores. Although difficult, if we stay the course and focus on the children, we will prevail.

Throughout the years there have been many attempts to implement real education reform. These innovations however, stalled and died not only due to the dramatic effort needed for implementation but due to political obstruction. The effort to thwart these great ideas went well beyond the politicians. It included corporations, think tanks, and other politically motivated organizations as well as a wide range of deceivers.

It was clearly not in their political and financial interest to abandon the failed ways of the past. As long as they could convince an unwitting public that their way was the best way, they could maintain their power, ego, and control as well as their financial success. To accomplish their goals, they took trickery and deceit to a new level.

Today's challenge is to expose the rhetoric of reform and replace it with real, whole child reform. To subtly maintain the status quo, charter schools were presented by the agenda driven politicians as their solution for a failed education system. Under the guise of innovation, many simply took the current system of public education and enhanced the failed methods of the past.

For students, simply changing schools didn't accomplish anything. Change must be connected to innovation to be effective.

Traditional public schools did no better, not because they didn't want to, because they were forced into a failed system that was never designed for all children. No Child Left Behind, Common Core and other failed mandates, driven by a one size fits all mentality, kept public schools in a box. They then had to go to the dark side to maintain their school thus leaving real innovation in the lurch.

## EXPOSING THE RHETORIC OF REFORM

To truly reform education, we must understand that current efforts are disguised to give the perception of innovation. The advent of charter schools, although well intended, brought every "sleight of hand" con artist out of the woodwork to promote their agenda rather than the agenda of children. Critical thinking then disappeared under the fog of deception, washed to the sea by those who believe in the power of word games and math riddles.

*Those innovative charters and traditional schools that are creative are pushed into anonymity by the sleight of hand experts who think they know how to run a school simply because they've been in one.*

### Follow the Money

Entrenchment and the lackluster effort toward change are not only supported by the unwillingness to improve the way we educate students, but also by many other major obstacles. For example, as reported by the Huffington Post, the National Board of Educational Testing and Public Policy at Boston College reported that the value of the standardized testing market was anywhere between $400 million and $700 million. And that does not include wraparounds and test prep.

"As of 2015, parents spent 13.1 billion on test prep that included preparation, tutoring and yes, counseling." Not to mention the money in the school testing budget. Consider the billions of dollars now wasted on meaningless testing which could go directly to schools to provide the strong, creative education to serve all students.

The battle to overcome the huge obstacles standing in the way of change will be difficult. Testing and textbook companies will fight it with every fiber of their being. Their livelihood is at stake and they have the money to mount an enormous campaign against educational concepts that don't support their financial interests. In this dastardly business driven by profits, the agenda of children has been lost.

According to the United States Department of Education, "the President requested $59 billion in discretionary appropriations for the Department of Education in fiscal year 2018, a $9 billion or 13% reduction below the 2017 annualized Continuing Resolution level. The request includes $1.4 billion to support new investments in public and private school choice.

With these cuts it is no surprise that urban schools lose much of their student population due to dropouts. Massive failure is driven by a testing system that forces those who learn in different ways and/or at different rates into an endless cycle of failure. This leads to their abandonment of any prospect of success. Eventually they drop out of school into a world of the unknown, forced to survive by any means necessary. And the schools get blamed.

Fueling the fire the current education system is dependent on drop-outs to save money by limiting the number of students attending school, while the penal system, however, has dramatically increased their budgets. According to the US Department of Education "State and local spending on prisons and jails has increased at triple the rate of funding for public education for preschool through grade 12 in the last three decades."

This doesn't make sense. Although the cost of education would increase dramatically if every child went to school for the full twelve years, the cost to run the penal system would drop. Politicians clearly don't want that.

## Strategies to Maintain the Status Quo

To maintain the status quo a variety of tactics are utilized. Those agenda driven politicians dig deep into their bag of tricks to assure the appearance of success where none exists. Every effort is made to make students, as well as parents comfortable with the current artificial school design.

Students who are deemed successful receive grandiose awards and recognition for gains made under the current system. These students are the unwitting foot soldiers leading the way into battle to maintain a system of education designed to support the massive testing industry. They point to these successes to convince citizens how great the system is.

Sadly, these "successful students" are manipulated into believing that they are prepared for the future. Little do they realize that when they get into the real world they need a completely different set of skills to function effectively. Yet those in power remain in opposition to systemic change, not because it isn't needed, but because they can sneak and connive, convincing an unwitting public that it isn't needed. Look at all the award-winning geniuses there are.

With dramatic failure in the current shattered system of education, the need for systematic change becomes essential. With every passing day, many students are dropping out while others are muddling through as unnoticed failures, never to receive necessary knowledge or skills. Less noticeable is the effort that drives children and then adults away from critical thinking.

The status quo must not continue to be maintained simply for the convenience of doing what has always been done. This dramatic transformation of schools now becomes an absolute necessity. No longer can students be allowed to be swallowed up by a dysfunctional system. No longer can memorized facts replace the ability to demonstrate a skill. No longer can taxpayer money be flushed down the toilet to fund such a futile endeavor.

We are about to embark on a monumental task. It will take every last ounce of energy to implement such a massive undertaking. Convincing the throngs of the need for this change is an enormous challenge. Reality dictates that it will be difficult for many to understand the necessity to develop this advanced educational system and philosophy.

However, times have changed and even the successful are shortchanged by the outdated educational process. Let those who succeed faster advance their skills when they are ready. Let those who succeed slower have more time to show their true abilities. But let them all gain usable knowledge necessary to prosper in a competitive world. Let them all be prepared to follow their pathway to success to become good, well-educated citizens.

## MAINTAING THE SUBCLASS

Trickery and deceit is a way of life for the agenda driven politicians as they have found ways to maintain the subclass, keeping children in their designated place in a social cast system by manipulating the educational process. Listening to the old worn out phrases gives a hint as to the antiquated thinking used in today´s educational world. "If the school day was longer kids would learn more, or unions are the problem or just raise the bar, or change to a charter school and the problem is solved." The reality is that none of these artificial changes make a difference.

The elevating of the artificial standardized test to celestial predominance becomes a smoke screen designed to assure a simplistic approach to education. The schools that have the best test scores win, regardless of the individual gains made by students in that school or what skills those students can demonstrate.

Little consideration is given to those children who have huge obstacles in the way of learning as they are expected to be proficient on the same day and at the same time as demanded by the standards. When those students don't "succeed" on the test like those in selected elite schools, their schools are deemed failures.

## HOW THEY JUSTIFY THE RACE

While some schools find creative ways to enroll the highest scoring students, those with special needs as well as those who are overwhelmed by poverty are left to the traditional public schools. And then they question why those schools are "failed" under artificial standards. Why aren't their students proficient at the same time and in the same place? Why can't students with special needs be proficient on the test?

Of course, there is a wide range of special needs as every child is different. However, reports of children leaving the test, crying because they couldn't read the questions are not exaggerated. Those who don't understand this must educate themselves. Those who do understand it and still force children into those situations must be removed from power. The time for action is now!

We must recognize the fundamental "problem at the bottom" is an outdated system of education that was never designed to serve all children. This is a system that Thomas Jefferson used to rake his geniuses and discard the rest. When we recognize that children are different and progress at different rates and learn in different ways, then and only then will we stop trying to rake those geniuses, determined by test scores, and begin to understand that there is a form of genius in everyone just waiting to come out.

When we stop viewing education as a race where all students must be at the same place at the same time under an outdated system, we will begin the process of whole child reform. It is time to realize the purpose of education is not to win, but to learn.

Educators understand the fundamental purpose of education is to prepare children for their future but that is not in the best interest of the agenda driven politicians. They need education to be a race so they can manipulate the public into believing their schools are first.

Of course, as letter grades often differ not only from city to city but from school to school and classroom to classroom, they are a great tool of deception. If you want your school to have a higher cumulative grade point average, you can, of course push out those with lower grades but why bother, just lower the standards to raise everyone's grades. That's how the game is played.

An example of grade inflation is when High School administrators would gather around the computer with their colleagues on the day grades were given. They would then bring up the records of athletes from various high schools who were ineligible due to low grade point averages and watch their grades move up one at a time until they were all eligible. Bets were taken as to whose grade would move up next. That's the very reason that the politicians froth at the mouth when they talk about grade point averages or test scores. They can control which of their crony schools would be successful.

The standard is not that students can think it's that they can score. The more we teach to the test, the higher they score and the less we allow students to think. To achieve school success, a new level of cheating must occur, and many administrators have become real professionals in that effort.


## THE HIGHLY-HONED SKILL OF CHEATING

Years back, because of poor test performance, the Birmingham Alabama district was in danger of being taken over by the state, so the people in charge did the most expedient thing. According to the late Steve Orel of the World of Opportunity School, 522 high school students were pushed out just before the test was administered.

Poor achieving students would now simply not be there to take the test thus raising the test score average. In an interesting contrast the Atlanta Public School's version of cheating had teachers simply erase the wrong test answers of the students and replaced them with the correct ones, thus increasing the schools test score average, all in the name of competition. But this is only the beginning of the trickery.

It's the proactive cheating that has been in place for years that goes unnoticed but is of greater concern. Let's go back to "old school cheating." In the good old days, when standardized tests were becoming significant, schools would become creative to assure only high scoring students took the test. One of the tricks was to give low scoring students a vacation on the day of the test.

They weren't suspended because that would show up on their records. They were just given a "time out." Parents were asked to keep their children home just for one day. "It would be difficult for them to take the test" parents were told. Make it easier for everyone. Students with special needs were easy targets for this type of deceptions. That kind of trickery should not be allowed in any school.

If this didn't work for some children, a different approach was taken. They would receive an official suspension keeping them home on testing day while administrators hoped that no one would check the records. Parents were kept in the dark and usually didn't complain because it took months for the test results to return and by then all was forgotten.

But now we get to the hardline students who weren't going to do well on the test but were also disruptive in school. This takes a greater effort and teamwork to assure those children were counted on the roles for the school to receive their required money but off the records when it came to test scores. In a large urban system, this turned into a game of "pass the student."

At the beginning of the year the student would remain on the roles until the official count was in and the school was assured the money. The student received an administrative removal shortly thereafter. That began a rotation from one school to another with yet another administrative removal from the receiving school until they ran out of schools. The strangeness of this was that the original school would receive one new student for every student they sent out, and that student often had more problems than the student dismissed from the school in the first place.

For some, the resolution for this problem was to keep the student's moving and keep them suspended while others could avoid enrolling those students altogether. That was especially valuable for charters as it was easier for them to push out students.

## The Farce of Graduation Rates

With competition, a long-standing indicator of success is the graduation rate of the school. How many students graduate on time. This is the biggest farce and the easiest to manipulate. Your school will be judged based on graduation rates so you want to make that data look the best possible. To graduate, school officials must hand the student a diploma, and that's it! Even if a test is required, this can be overcome through a little fancy paper-work.

Here's a real-life example concerning a young girl with special needs. Mary (not her real name), a student with special needs, graduated from middle school, went to high school for three years and dropped out per her older sister who raised her. On graduation day, low and behold there goes Mary, walking across the stage receiving a full diploma. That was not only unethical as it was designed to make the school look good, it was illegal under special education laws. But it was daily practice. Of course, graduation rates go up if you can pull off this scam.

We now come upon the age old alternative school scam. Schools send their low scoring students to a warehouse style alternative school and keep the high scoring ones for bragging rights. This is evidenced by the Olympia school in Orlando Florida who pride themselves on a 90 percent graduation rate.

According to an article in ProPublica, written by Hannah Fresques and Heather Vogell, entitled Alternative Education: Using Charter Schools to Hide Drop Outs to Game the System: "Olympia keeps its graduation rate above 90 percent—and its rating an "A" under Florida's all-important grading system for schools—partly by shipping its worst achievers to Sunshine (alternative school)."

More and more schools are coming under scrutiny as many have a policy of trickery and deceit to scam the system to be perceived as better than they are. A complaint was filed by the Latino Coalition of New Jersey, a Monmouth and Ocean counties advocacy group, and Fair Schools Red Bank, a local organization supportive of the district's traditional public schools. They said the Red Bank Charter School failed to comply with a consent order from the Commissioner of Education regarding diverse enrollment. Picking and choosing their students is a well-known strategy.

The Coalition for Community Schools New Orleans (CCS) is an alliance of parent, youth and community organizations and labor groups fighting for educational justice and equity in access to school resources and opportunities. Their report, "System Failure: Louisiana's Broken Charter School Law" cites billions of taxpayer dollars plunged into charter schools since Hurricane Katrina hit, including over $831 million in the 2014–15 school year alone.

According to the New Orleans Tribune, "local education advocate Karran Harper Royal, who is a part of the Coalition for Community Schools, says the hope is that with the release of this report, the state will both tighten its controls over the financial management of charter schools, making them more accountable to parents, children and taxpayers, and review its approach to academic accountability."

According to the report 2005, charter school enrollment in the state has grown 1,188 percent. The Louisiana Department of Education's Recovery School District, originally created to facilitate state takeover of struggling schools, is now the first charter-only school district in the country. Under their leadership, a school that fails to make required academic improvement is either closed completely or re-opened by another charter operator. It is a process that advocates say is hurting children.

*Some charter schools are better and some are worse, but rarely are they different*

Every time a school is closed, the students, with their parents, struggle to find a new school. This school is often a further distance away creating a significant inconvenience. The question remains, will the new school be better, or just slicker in their marketing efforts. According to the Coalition report, "The state's academic oversight system relies largely on sets of data that can be manipulated by regulators, authorizers, or the charters themselves. Without reliable data, schools, parents, and the public have no way to accurately gauge academic quality at their schools."

The ability to avoid students with low achievement records is still a highly honed skill. Even utilizing something as simple as a lottery to determine those who would enter a highly desirable school would be available for deceit if one so chooses. Here is the downside to that. Although everyone interested in the school would sign up for the lottery, it is possible, for those with evil intent, to make the sign-up process difficult for those parents who worked two or three jobs to survive. There is always an angle if one chooses to use it.

## But We Aren't Certified to Take "Those" Children

A major target for those who want a controlled school environment is to find excuses not to serve students with special education needs. The traditional public schools often have the resources to serve these students and are not allowed to reject them, while charters, choice, and others make it clear that they aren't allowed to serve them.

This issue could be resolved with a little teamwork if school personnel were truly concerned about all children. A teacher certified in special education, while hired by the traditional public school, could be assigned to a charter school in a cooperative effort. This also goes for any personnel needed to fulfill Federal and State regulations related to the students Individual Education Plan.

The time has come to focus on the education of children rather than the agenda driven rhetoric that is happening throughout the political spectrum. Simply by switching from traditional public schools, to private schools, to pseudo public charter schools does nothing to change the way we educate children. The system and philosophy of education must change in order to see students serviced in a meaningful way.

It is abundantly clear that systemic change, coming from on high, will not occur in the near future. However, there is always hope as long as good teachers are in the classroom. When that classroom door closes, or when teachers venture into the community with their students, it is their class and they are in control. The testing police can't be everywhere. It is time to do a little sneaking and conniving of our own to assure all of our children can get the best whole child education possible.

Systemic change, from the ground up will be the most difficult challenge ever attempted by educators. We begin by infusing and embedding innovative ideas into the "normal" curriculum.

*It is time for teachers to drive the engine of change. No longer may we allow politicians to destroy kids for their political advantage.*

# Chapter 4

# Infiltrating the Curriculum

Efforts to hold children hostage by controlling the curriculum must be quashed for thinking and creativity to work their way back into the educational process. It is time for teachers to break out of those shackles and free the children to follow their dreams down their pathway to success. For teachers to accomplish the freedom to teach, they must realize that they still control their classes. Welcome to the devious world of the angry child advocates. The advocates who will no longer sit back and tolerate children being treated like robots.

*Here we empower teachers to subtly change the system from the bottom up. In this chapter is a range of ideas, justified, to teach the whole child. Take as many as you want and make them your own.*

In the new world view, children will not only be allowed to think, but think critically and rationally. That should be scary to many politicians as those adults will now find children threatening to the power base they are losing. Only by manipulating children have they been able to hold on to their power. Only by holding children hostage have they been able to hold control over the world of education.

Let the games begin. The solution to many of the educational concerns is to incorporate those classes that have been eliminated by the reformers into the everyday curriculum. The reality is most of these activities provide skills that go well beyond those seen on the surface.

Let us begin with the arts. If you try to explain the importance of the arts to politicians or those of the corporate board rooms, they will turn a deaf ear. However, if you utilize your skills in trickery and deceit for the good of children, you will broaden the area of reading and writing to one that includes all the well accepted communication skills such as reading, writing, listening, sign language, foreign language, speaking, and performing. Everyone knows communication skills are important and are unlikely to reject them. Wait a minute; was performing listed as a communication skill? Don't tell anyone but "the arts" just made it to the mainstream.

## INFILTRATING THE CURRICULUM; THE ARTS

The arts have been a mainstay in societies throughout the world and through-out history. They are not only used for the aesthetic value but for a means of communication. If you look at everything from rap and folk music to classical and pop the artist tells a story about them and their community. The concerns are expressed just as if they were written or given in a speech.

Going back 40,000 years, there is proof that the first musical instruments existed. At that time, according to the documentary on PBS, "Great Human Odyssey," "Music and Art became the building blocks of a shared culture that the Neanderthals lacked," Homo Sapiens brought with them imagination. "We plan, we think, we imagine, we innovate, we had the ability to commu-nicate" and that is why many believe Homo Sapiens thrived and live today, and Neanderthals perished. Music and the arts were the glue that kept society together. Stories were told, ideas were exchanged, drawings on cave walls told of events of the time and the human race was born. That is powerful!

As the artists draw a mural on a wall in the community or in the school, a message of hope is sent to all who see it. The paintings of Picasso, Rem-brandt, Da Vinci, and Monet bring their beauty and thoughts to the canvas. Martha Graham was quoted as saying "Dance is the hidden language of the soul of the body." A message is sent every time a dancer sets foot on a stage. A simple song "Give Peace a Chance" by John Lennon was a strong state-ment for the peace movement in the seventies. "We shall Overcome" was the rallying cry of the freedom movement of the sixties.

"Oh Freedom" was a statement made by the Igbo tribe from Southern Nigeria as they refused to enter the new world as slaves, instead they walked into the water to "take them home" to a better place. The message there was "Before I'd be a slave I'll be buried in my grave and go home to my Lord and be free." That message evolved from the Igbo Landing in 1803 and resonated for more than two centuries to tell the story of their quest for freedom.

What better way to take you through an emotional journey than a sym-phony telling a story through music? Tchaikovsky's 1812 overture, complete with cannons, tells the story of Napoleon's retreat from Russia in 1812 while John Philip Sousa ignites the patriotism in this country with his marches. Katharine Lee Bates along with Woody Guthrie tell this country's story for all to hear. The beautiful ballet Swan Lake by Tchaikovsky tells the story of Odette, a princess turned into a swan by an evil sorcerer's curse. The music cultivates the imagination and stirs the heart. This tradition must continue.

As Shakespeare developed his plays, a story was told not once but throughout the centuries. Plays are developed not only for the pleasure, although that does enhance the quality of life, they also tell a wide variety of stories. The social statement made in West Side Story is brought to life and will be for many years. This social commentary is still relevant today.

## A Voice That Won't Be Silenced

Plays were shut down in many countries when they were provocative in nature in the eyes of the dictators, yet they kept on persisting. "The Suicide" in 1928 was written by Nikolai Erdman. It talked about Russians taking back their lives from Communism. It took Stalin one performance to understand what it advocated, and he banned it. It continued playing on under the name "Dying for It" and could not be silenced.

An article in Soundscapes.info entitled "Popular music and processes of social transformation" by Peter Wick stated, "The power of rock music thus derived from the impossibility—at least for politicians—of conceptualizing its ideological content, from the fact that it could survive independently of any form of material embodiment, and from the fact that public performances were difficult in the extreme for the authorities to control."

Against this background, and understanding the real influence of mass reactions in a unified state system and the very real fear of it that existed in the minds of political leaders, it becomes easy to understand why the most popular rock musicians in fact possessed considerable political power. This was a power, therefore, that state authorities could not ignore. Neither was it a power that could be arbitrarily repressed."

Artists can be stopped but their music and their plays, their art and their radio and television presentations cannot. Pete Seeger was blacklisted from performing, especially on television because his song "Waist Deep in the Big Muddy" talked about the Vietnam War. Tom and Dick Smothers had him on their show anyway and later quit the show due to restrictions demanded of them by the network. But Seeger's music carried on to this day. Paul Robison was blacklisted everywhere in the United States, so he went to foreign countries where he was treated like a king, so the US government took away his passport. They may have stopped him for a time, but his music and thoughts continue to this day.

*"As an artist I come to sing, but as a citizen, I will always speak for peace, and no one can silence me in this." —Paul Robison*

The arts alone make a strong contribution as they provide relief from the drudgery of everyday life and in schools where they energize the student body. Learning not only becomes an enjoyable experience but one that enhances the whole child.

Whether it's a vocation or avocation, the whole child needs the type of fulfillment offered by the arts. A rocker from Austin Texas makes his living with music but once he puts the brush to the canvas, his genius unfolds. Bob Schneider makes a good living with his music yet enjoys his art. Lilli K tells us "don't steal the magic" of women. Cal and Margie Adams tell their story through songs that he wrote.

Victoria Lee wrote, produced and acted in the web movie "Low Strung" which shows the diversity of Chicago's millennials. Rhiannon Giddens tells of the long journey on the freedom highway, all in music. And she also brings back bluegrass roots and the banjo to its rightful place in Black History. They say the arts are not communication skills necessary for life?

The arts can awaken the soul of those who have so much to offer. Albert Einstein was literally told he was too stupid to learn. His mother didn't accept that and pulled him out of school. She bought young Albert a violin which he played continuously. From that day forward, Einstein was a changed man. To the day he died, Einstein insisted that the reason for his success was that he played the violin. According to G. J. Withrow, his lifetime friend, Einstein worked on his theories while improvising on the violin. It helped him think.

Einstein's wife Elsa once remarked, "I fell in love with Albert because he played Mozart so beautifully on the violin. He also plays the piano. Music helps him when he is thinking about his theories. He goes to his study, comes back, strikes a few chords on the piano, jots something down, returns to his study."

In the everyday communications curriculum, every mode of communication must be utilized. But the arts are not limited to the communications curriculum. They are also essential to history, philosophy, motor skills, spatial skills, critical thinking, and a wide variety of other skills essential to the future of children. For the politicians, calling the class Communication Skills is sufficient. Sneak it into the curriculum, not necessarily as a class but as a strong part of a curriculum. If classes in the arts will be allowed, all the better.

By eliminating the arts in schools, an entire culture of communication is silenced. Is that not the goal of the agenda driven politicians? Is that not necessary to maintain their power, ego, and control?

## Integrating the Arts with History

Throughout history, the arts have been a mainstay in the process of communication. The history of the world can easily be found in the songs, the writings, the paintings, in dance, and the list goes on. From paintings on a cave wall to a play, to an opera, to the songs of Pete Seeger, Bob Dylan, and the New Freedom Singers, stories have been told. Now it is time for the students to have that experience.

Here is an example of integrating the arts based on the study of the History of slavery:

- A student will write or perform a song or a rap.
- A student will paint a mural on the school wall.
- A student will participate in a debate, forensic activity, or a speech.
- A student will perform and/or choreograph a dance.
- A student will write and/or perform in a play.
- A student will design clothes and/or coordinate a fashion show.

Presenting in the form of an exhibition or a demonstration of learning gives students the latitude to choose their own personal way to demonstrate what they have learned and thus the probability of success will increase dramatically. Here is a sample lesson plan designed to incorporate music and theater into the history curriculum.

Objective: Students will be able to describe a specific turning point in the history of slavery in the United States.

- Students will individually research and outline the history of slavery in the United States.
- Working in teams, students will decide a point in history for their focus.
- Students will research songs from that era. Follow the Drinking Gourd; Oh Freedom; Song of the Free; The Good Old Way and We Shall Overcome are examples.
- Students, as a chorus, will learn and perform the song of their choosing.
- Students will work in small groups to develop and present a short skit incorporating the song.
- A video of the skit will be played, and a discussion will follow.

This area of study is rich with musical thoughts that allow students to feel the history rather than just read about it. A much better understanding of history will be the result. This is only one example. Think of the many other ways of utilizing musicians, dancers, visual artists, and others to enhance the education of all students. There is a wealth of talent in the community, use it.

*Seek out music teachers wherever you can find them. Bring the professionals into your school and incorporate music into every possible part of the curriculum.*

# INFILTRATING THE CURRICULUM;
# THE JOY OF READING

The current mandated system of education often insists on artificial learning emphasizing rigor. But that is just code for meaningless drivel that demands a constant "shoulder to the grindstone" approach to learning what you are told, regardless of the significance of the lesson. Reading is personal and must begin with the student's background knowledge and then expand to the stars and beyond.

Children are not standardized therefore learning should not be standardized. To develop reading skills, first students must be able to read much of what is put in front of them, and it must mean something to them. Take children step by step, until the light bulb goes off then reading becomes everyday business. The materials used must be high interest for them as well as at their reading level or slightly above. As they develop confidence, reading levels move up and up. And as they develop the joy of reading, they will begin to read everything in sight.

## Reading Clubs

"Reading Clubs" is a concept designed for every child to learn at their best rate. For students, we call them what they are, Reading Clubs. For the agenda driven politicians we can call it a supplemental reading program. To assure acceptance we can inform them that it supports grit and although children are miserable, they are learning whether they want to or not. A little white lie is alright when we are supporting children.

Like the concept of "stop everything and read" the entire school stops classes for forty-five minutes on a regular basis. Every educator in the building becomes a reading teacher to assure small class sizes. No letter grades are given and there is no competition. Students are assigned to the levels of their assessment and adjusted by teachers who see differences within the groups. Here is how it plays out:

A student we will call Sonny, entered a middle school as a seventh grader. He was placed in reading clubs and given a one on one, non-threatening simple test to determine which club he would be in. He scored on the pre-primer level which was confirmed by his classroom teacher and we moved forward.

Teachers don't brow beat kids, they don't tell them they are stupid with a letter grade and most of all, they don't have them compete in any way. Never, ever will reading clubs knock the joy of learning out of them. Students were in groups reading high interest articles but with words they could read. There is no interest in giving them a seventh-grade text if they read at a third-grade level. There is no interest in shaming them into learning. With a "one on one" pre-and post-assessment, teachers can stay on top of progress and it is not, in any way intimidating to the students.

There is a myth that students would be embarrassed and would act out if they were in low skill groups but that didn't happen. During the reading club (classes) you could hear a pin drop in the school. Why, because they could actually read the articles given. Secondly, class sizes were determined by reading levels. Low skill students had very small class sizes and as we got to those on a higher level, the sizes increased. Those beyond their level had even larger sizes. You will simply never get low scoring children to read in a mob. Class size is essential. And finally, the culture of the school emphasized learning rather than winning.

Now did Sonny miraculously jump up seven grade levels and read into the twilight? No, in fact for the first three months he wouldn't even look at a book. Until one day he was walking in the hallway when spotted by an administrator. Before being admonished for being in the hall he shouted "When will we have reading clubs again?" The administrator stopped cold, shocked by this unexpected behavior. "Do you like reading club?" "Yes," he said and ran off. Now for the non-believers, this is a true story.

Due to the individual attention and patience of his teacher, Mark Jabir, the light bulb went off. Hearing him in the hall constantly pestering his teacher as to when the next reading club would be, was music to my ears. And the result was that he gained four grade levels during the remainder of that school year along with the following year. Remember, this is a young man who gained nothing in the previous six years.

This is an individual example of how reading clubs supported children in developing reading skills and it didn't cost a penny more! We must give children the power to learn, to use their brains to discover and analyze rather than memorize. They must learn to find their way in life, as leaders down their pathway of success rather than followers only to falter when they splash into the real world of work, community involvement, and daily living.

Greater gains will happen, not necessarily in the next year but maybe the following year and sometimes later. If we stay with students, they will succeed. Today the pattern is to push them out of school before they have a chance to blossom. Pressure them into their own "suicide by street" and watch the cycle of poverty play out as the system continues as its purpose of maintaining the subclass.

The reality is that through the reading clubs, individual expectations are high, and standards become guidelines for success rather than deadlines for failure. This of course would lead to individualized schools which are necessary for that success. The main difference between this new system and the current one is that this one never gives up on students. An individualized school with no false letter grades, no artificial grade levels, and a failure system that is part of the learning process will serve all students well.

When the reading club concept was put in place at the school, reading levels were not prominently displayed. Students merely went to Ms. Brown's room or Mr. Collins' room to read. Most important of all is that students became more concerned with their learning rather than their level. With the proper school atmosphere, as well as anonymity, the concept of learning exceeded the concept of winning and education became real. Here's how it was done:

- An atmosphere of respect was encouraged by every staff member.
- Student confidentiality was maintained. When students went to reading class, they went to "Ms. Brown's room" or "Mr. Collins' room"; it was just another class.
- Reading materials, although on grade levels, did not indicate anywhere what level they were except for coded messages to teachers. Teachers did not discuss it in public.

The implementation of the reading clubs was as follows:

- The reading groups met three times during the week for a forty-five-minute period.
- The reading-group monitor was either a teacher, student teacher, Principal, counselor, a social worker, a psychologist, or other educator.
- The students read trade books, articles, newspapers, plays, or for pleasure, and learned about new topics.
- Each group had methods for documentation, discussion, and review.
- As student's progressed, these reading groups changed to meet the needs of the students.
- Teachers provided the reading materials for each group at the specific level needed.
- The first five minutes of each reading club session gave the students an introduction to the reading material, and allowed them to discuss difficult new vocabulary words.
- Finally, the reading took place.

Depending on the size of the group, a variety of methods were used to assure each student had sufficient reading time. With ten minutes remaining in the session, the teacher or a student conducted a discussion of the reading. With five minutes remaining the students documented their participation.

Call it reading class or reading supplement, but never ever call it the joy of reading in front of the agenda driven politicians. Only in front of the children.

## INFILTRATING THE CURRICULUM;
## IN THE COMMUNITY

Ingenuity allows educators to simply ignore the politicians and move ahead with what is best to prepare their children for the future. There is no rule that says the class must be held within the school. Therefore, it is not necessary to sneak around to do this activity. Where are your kids? They're in class of course.

As we move the class out of the building, we must keep in mind one fundamental issue; never, ever is there a community experience where students are simply set free to catch education in a bushel basket. Every minute of every day is planned for learning, connected to the overall lesson plan as well as the specific target proficiencies of the individual student. Now we are free to walk out the front door to seek teachable moments wherever we can find them.

An activity that might be more acceptable to those who are agenda driven is collaboration with businesses. To make learning real, it must begin at the front door of the school and move outward to wherever it takes us. As students explore the neighborhood, they become cognizant of the numerous companies that exist in their community. From these companies the students choose who will be educational partners.

### Beginning at the Front Door

Especially when given large blocks of time within the schedule, taking students into the community as well as bringing community members into the school leads to quality teachable moments. The journey begins by mapping the neighborhood, diagramming streets as well as identifying businesses in the area. Most amazing is the number of businesses in the immediate vicinity that are willing to support schools with their thoughts and actions.

We begin with the selection of business partners, no longer those chosen for their financial contributions to schools, but those who can contribute based on the needs of students to learn and thrive in their community. The activities are planned, coordinated, and conducted by students. Students in leadership roles empower them to think, explore, and make decisions under the guidance of the teacher. This is a far cry from answering questions on a test. Paul Simon sang "I look back on all the crap I learned in high school. It's a wonder I can think at all." The song "Kodachrome" tells the story simply and quite well.

The future of education must allow kids to think, and support both with corrections and acceptance. Let them learn from failure rather than just fail from failure. Guaranteed, students will remember these experiences and the lessons they provide.

To allow for specific examples the experiences at the Milwaukee Village School, a traditional public school founded by this author and partner Mary Gale Budzisz, will be utilized. The need to develop good reading skills in all students is of great concern to every school. To this end, we looked to the neighborhood for a local bookstore as a partner. Carla Allison and her Readers Choice bookstore became a phenomenal partner to the Milwaukee Village School.

Not only were kids introduced to books by visiting her store, many projects were developed through Carla's participation at the school. Students were introduced to entrepreneurship and taught how to develop a business. They also developed a book club, getting a grant to purchase books from the store to support student reading at every level.

One of the most exciting partnerships was the school's relationship with farmer Will Allen. Interested students learned in Will's greenhouse by growing food, nurturing it, and passing it on to those in the community. This whole concept began with an effort to beautify the neighborhood. The student in charge of beautifying the local day care took phone calls from local officials or community members about that project. And the calls went to the student, not to a staff member.

Students were put in the lead. From this beginning, Will developed Growing Power Inc. and became an international authority educating people on the value of good nutrition and quality food. Our students blossomed in that setting, not through taking a test but by real learning and getting their hands dirty in the worm tank.

Think of all the possibilities that will occur with the help of creative partnerships. Milwaukee Village School had relationships with programs like the Black Health Coalition that led to students planning and fully developing an anti-smoking campaign including running a conference.

A partnership with MATA Media, the local public-access television station, had students take part in a great English lesson around a public service announcement that went on the air. The AODA, a program to get kids away from alcohol and drugs had the kids boarding a bus in Milwaukee to go to Boston to see the whales, a trip that the students chose. Teachable moments were everywhere on that trip and the bus was the classroom.

Upon visiting a business, it is important to assure all students are fully prepared. They do research to determine the history of the business as well as significant information about the business. The intent is not simply to walk through and listen to the presentations by the business representatives; it is also to prepare questions to further their knowledge. Here's the plan for full student involvement and critical thinking:

## Understanding Business, First Hand

Objective: To allow students the opportunity to visit local businesses and interview the personnel to better understand the inner workings of that business.

Have students make a list entitled "Local Businesses" on large paper to post on classroom wall.

- Students create an interview form; brainstorming what information should be on the form; developing the learning objective.
- Create small student teams and have each team choose a business.
- Role-play the interview process; teach social skills needed for this project, such as listening, asking a question, and saying "thank-you."
- Have each student team call its business and set up an interview time.
- Students explain what they are doing.
- Students create a calendar of their business interview times/dates.
- During the interview, students work together to fill out the form.
- Video and/or photo documentation can be included with business personnel permission.
- Students note their own participation in their journal for future reference.
- Each student team prepares an oral presentation about their business.
- Document all career possibilities on the large paper after each team presentation.
- Have each student prepare an essay about what they learned during their team interviews.

There are several examples why this traditional public neighborhood school was ideal for blending the community into the school for the highest quality educational experience. When students go on a community experience in the neighborhood, it is their neighborhood they would "discover." They live in the neighborhood so when they map that neighborhood looking for businesses as partners, they might very well pass their house. Students then take the lead and introduce their teachers and classmates to the family and friends that run the businesses.

Here is an example of a community-based learning experience that utilizes a business partner. The partner is a local public-access television station. The subjects covered are reading in the research of the activity, writing as students prepare the script and acting/speaking as students appear in front of the camera to deliver the finalized announcement. Technology skills are taught as students learn to use the equipment. Individual goals are developed with students assigned, based on their needs.

## Public Service Announcement, the English Lesson (PSA)

What better way to bring back the joy of learning than by putting students in front of a television camera. Middle school students are "on stage" as part of their nature, so it is best to use the "ham" in them to their educational advantage. Again, the joy of learning comes to the forefront. Every minute is planned to assure the students maximum success toward their educational goals.

Objective: To provide a hands-on approach to television production while gaining real-life skills. This provides an opportunity for students to prepare an announcement that will be televised to the whole community. This experience was blended into a wide range of academic skills as confirmed by the following lesson plan.

- Students research problems particular to their own community. This includes individual research as well as group activity.
- Each group involved chooses a topic: violence, drugs, smoking, child abuse, litter, malnutrition, dropouts, or safety are some examples.
- Students watch, and critique various sample announcements previously used.
- Students brainstorm about what message to give to the public about the chosen topic.
- Students prepare the script/message.
- Students practice and critique themselves as they develop their presentations.
- Students prepare for their visit to the television studio by contacting the administrator.
- The students practice proper communication skills to use in the business setting of the TV studio.
- The students visit the television studio and learn about cameras, lighting, sound boards, and floor-manager duties from the staff.
- After the initial presentation by the studio staff, students return to school to decide what specific job they would like to do to achieve the goal of a completed public service announcement. Usually the job they choose is consistent with their strengths, abilities, and interests.
- Students are involved in the entire production, including many different takes when shooting the scene, editing, voice-overs, and preparation for showing.
- PSAs are then shown on the local public-access TV station.

This is quite an adventure when consideration is given to the wide range of academic subjects covered in this real-life experience. It is significant that the skills necessary are aligned with the skills of the student, so they will improve their academics in an effective manner. Every minute is a learning experience. It is amazing that when students learn reading, for example, in a real-life setting, their mastery of words increases as they can put them in a proper context.

There is, of course, much more to connecting with the community than teaming with businesses. Connecting with friends, relatives, seniors, and a wide range of neighbors advances the partnership with the school and increases learning experiences for students. Imagine implementing these plans as part of your curriculum. If anyone asks, you are in the classroom. You would not be lying because in a community-based school, the classroom is the community.

## Knowing Your Neighbor

Regardless of what the politicians are told, there is a great deal of learning that is essential to daily life. The good news is that the fundamentals of reading and math are built into every adventure, and it isn't drudgery. The project we are about to embark on could have several different headings. Math, since students are measuring, history because they are telling the story of their neighborhood and even, with a little imagination, enhancing the skills necessary to be a surgeon by developing fine motor control sewing a quilt. Well, that may be a stretch, but the rest is fully legitimate and, of course, reading and writing are built in. And of most importance, creativity.

Objective: To create a quilt using individual material squares made by each student using ideas based on his/her own community.

The teacher explains the project and introduces quilt-making. Samples are brought, and the history of quilt-making is explored. Each student will start with one 9"×9" fabric square. Students determine the yardage of the material and cut the squares. They will start with one quilt per class. Part of the magic of quilting is the community aspect as all the squares are integrated into a whole product.

- Each student is to create a short story about something in his or her own neighborhood. Some examples are gardens, flowers, litter, people, stores, or community problems.
- Each student will depict the story in a drawing including a message.
- Each student transfers the drawing to the fabric square using fabric markers.
- Students create the story for the quilt (or quilts) by placing their fabric squares in a pattern.
- Students sew the squares together.
- Students cut the backing and attach it to their quilt.

- Students prepare a written story with their own group about their own quilt.
- Quilts can be given to nursing homes as lap blankets after quilts are displayed on the walls of school.

## Bringing In The Community

What better way to get to know your neighbors, business representatives, politicians, and other community leaders than to invite them in to talk to the students? All too often children grow into adults without knowing the roles or experiences of those in their neighborhood. The community school philosophy is to take the classroom into the community and bring the community members into the classroom to better understand a child's future role in their neighborhood. Help them learn what will be expected of them once successful. And just maybe, those neighbors will become advocates for the school.

Student-led activities bring community members into the school building to present or to simply connect with the students in social situations. Character development skills are taught as well as practiced ensuring a positive image when connecting with the visitors. Proper etiquette is used when students make phone calls, welcome the guests, introduce the guests, and are involved in all aspects of the visit.

Objective: To bring people of interest into the school to share their expertise with the students, and to expose the visitors to the positive climate of the school.

- With the students in the lead, they, along with teachers, create a list of possible visitors to invite.
- The students in each classroom decide whom to invite.
- The students draft and write an invitation letter explaining what they would like the visitor to teach or demonstrate.
- A yearly calendar is created to note who will be the Guest-of-the-Month.
- Each classroom teacher reviews appropriate social skills.
- The anticipatory set includes a discussion about the guest.
- Etiquette is reviewed and practiced through role-playing.
- Students prepare to document what they have learned from the guest.
- The host students organize the program and choose who will introduce the guest.
- Photos can be taken of the guest with host classroom students. A Photo Wall will be used to display the pictures.
- The teacher leads a classroom discussion about what they learned from the guest.
- All students write a thank-you note to the guest. The classroom hosts collect and mail the notes.

This next activity is designed to support the connection between students and the elderly. It is amazing what new perceptions are gained when the elders of the community sit down for a meal with polite young people in a school setting. This inter-generational nutrition program has been used successfully at the Milwaukee Village School. A whole new group of school supporters was born.

## Dining with the Elders

Everyone must eat lunch, they haven't banned that yet. Let's get sneaky and make that a learning experience. Throughout history community elders have played a major role in educating children. Why shouldn't this continue? What wealth of information will come from those who have lived in the neighborhood. The children then invite them to lunch to hear their stories.

Objective: To use information gathered from the survey method and act on the findings.

- Students conduct a survey to determine the needs in the neighborhood.
- Students conduct classroom discussions on how they can help address the issue, and each class elect's representatives for the core committee.
- With the guidance of the teacher, students are fully involved in writing a local district grant to fund the project.
- Students identify the elderly in the neighborhood to be invited. (Students attending neighborhood schools are all from the surrounding neighborhood so that is an additional advantage.)
- Invitations are carefully made by the students and hand-delivered to the respective elderly.
- Students research foods that provide nutritional value. Groups such as the Black Health Coalition are brought in as experts.
- Students write up menus which are nutritionally balanced.
- Students contact local caterers to supply the food paid for with grant funds.
- The grant funds local transportation for guests to and from the school.
- Students set up and decorate the lunch room.
- During the meal, students make introductions, serve the food, and provide the entertainment. They get to know their neighbors, and, of equal importance, their neighbors get to know them and appreciate their altruism.

It is important to recognize that student involvement in every aspect of a project will drive learning toward their proficiencies. Writing a good invitation, planning the menu, analyzing the costs, preparing a budget, organizing the guest list, preparing the room, serving the lunch, and socializing properly are the responsibilities of the students. These skills must be learned and honed as even many adults have not mastered the concepts.

Because of this nutrition project, students will become friends with the local elderly neighbors. The spin-off activities that evolve are coordinated by the students. The students will interview each of the elderly participants and ask them, "What can we do for you?" Students then adopt projects and provide community service.


## INFILTRATING THE CURRICULUM; EXPLORATORY WORKSHOPS

The current system and philosophy of education was designed to "rake a few geniuses from the rubbish." That led to an uneven playing field for students. Here is how a little trickery and deceit can open the doors to every child's dream. As we "even the playing field" for every student we must determine which students have the ability to take part in high skill-level jobs.

In the past, those with good grades in some subject areas would learn advanced skills. Grades being moot, it is time to allow students to tell educators what their interests are and how they want to achieve them. No longer may we push kids out of school before they blossom.

Here's how we get every child the chance to follow their dreams. We introduce students to high-level skills via exploratory workshops. These hands-on activities are two to three-week workshops giving students an idea of what goes into a profession of their interest. All students are welcomed regardless of their skills and abilities. It is important that we never again only seek students the school system deems worthy. We never know when genius will unfold, so we must allow it to happen.

The emphasis here is "hands on" wherever possible. When Dr. Temple Grandon speaks, she talks about the classes that saved her future. Dr. Grandon is autistic and considered a genius. Although autism is seen by many as an extreme disability, the reality is that, according to Dr. Grandon, in Silicon Valley, most CEO's are autistic to a degree. All brains are different. In the movie about her and in real life, she gives credit to her science teacher who got her involved in hands-on activities, working with her strengths. Shouldn't this be the same for every student?

These workshops will be available to all students, whenever they decide they are ready, and will be held throughout the year for designated periods of time with the intent of introducing students to specific high-level skills. For example, a workshop could be held in a profession that utilizes college-level physics such as research engineer which might last two to three weeks.

Remember, these are hands-on activities as much as possible. Individual schools develop their own specific time frames for the sessions. Some could be held in the evening, some in the morning before the regular school day starts, some during off time in a year-round schedule, or on weekends. These workshops would be scattered throughout the student's high-school years, utilizing the time frames of their entire high-school career to implement this essential part of the program.

Here are the fundamentals regarding how this would work in a high school:

• Students will be exposed to a specific high-level skill in exploratory workshops when they decide they are ready.
• Students will not receive a letter grade or credit for taking these classes. There would be no pass or failure. The class is informational for the student.
• Workshops will focus on "hands-on" skills needed for the various professions.
• From information gathered, the students would then determine if they are interested in pursuing any of these higher-level skills.
• Those pursuing higher-level skills will then enroll in those full credit classes when they are ready.

Of course, the workshops include visits to the experts in the community. This is a complete program of job exploration that requires higher-level skills. Students who have been labeled as slower will now have a chance to let their real talents show rather than keep them hidden under an obsolete discriminatory educational design. This is a student driven activity.

## INFILTRATING THE SYSTEM; IN NATURE

The environmental overnight camping trip is a phenomenal experience allowing educators to build in as many academics as possible, combining them with learning about the environment.

Urban systems can take the students to the wilderness while rural students can "camp" in the city. Camping could include spending the night in a university dorm or a safe outdoor location such as a zoo. This could bring a wide variety of experiences.

Wherever the students go, the classroom goes and so goes the lesson for the day. Seek out a teachable moment wherever one can be found. This involves "easy to find" partners such as the YMCA, Scouts, and others who manage campgrounds. Combined with parks and recreation centers there are always experts available with the knowledge that will help students understand the world we live in.

The teachable moments are many as students take over the wide range of responsibilities necessary for "survival" in an unknown environment. A simple hike in the woods at nighttime turns into an adventure trying to catch the elusive snipe, a small mythical feathered beast, friendly to mankind. Students, nervous with anticipation, prepared to leave on a late-night walk through the woods. Silly playing turned to silence as the "snipe" was described and our effort to catch this elusive critter planned.

Slowly we crept into the woods following what they didn't know was a predetermined path designed to allow for the sights and sounds of nature. The sound of rustling bushes had wide-eyed children wondering, what is it? Who is it following? Leading the pack of adventure seekers, I was quick to point out what appeared to be a nest of branches, a clear sign that the snipe was nearby.

A hush came over the crew as another rustling had this school leader, credibility in danger, diving headfirst into the nest, struggling with the largest of all snipe (that suspiciously looked to adults like a pile of leaves). Asking for assistance, only Sean came stumbling through the darkness to help as the rest looked on in anticipation. "I'm coming, I'm coming, I see it, I see its eyes," hollered Sean as he tripped over some branches and rolled toward the nest. Mysteriously, the snipe escaped just before he got there, leaving only a pile of leaves, but the sight of their administrator, covered from head to toe in mud, gave students a different view of their fearless leader.

Listening to the sounds of nature and other things that go bump in the night changes the perspective of those students. They let their guard down and the rough and tumble kids of the classroom turn into the children they really are. A scary story at night had one group of eleven-year-old children seemingly disappearing from their beds only to be found, all in one bed, huddling in semi-fear in the camaraderie they developed with their peers. The next morning begins with the routines of the camp followed by the environmental lessons of the day, within the environment that is real. And it's all in the "classroom."

## TEST PREP?

What about test prep? That will take a lot more creativity especially if the test police come around on a regular basis. If there continues to be a script to follow offered up by your state, make sure it is available on your desk always. It must be at arm's reach to assure you stay on script without wavering.

If the test police come in, you will be right on target on the right page at the right time, and right on cue, just as you prompted your students to respond. When the test police leave, you immediately go back to the reading clubs or whatever real activity you are involved in. It is unethical and even immoral to teach to the test following a script that only swallows up the minds of young people.

You must answer correctly when asked about data that is required to report to administrators. In that vein, you may have to spend a minimal amount of time teaching to the test. If you aren't on the same page at the same time required, and the testing police are requiring a report, give it to them honestly.

It doesn't matter to students if you are behind on the script as it is only damaging them and tearing them away from authentic education. If there are test scores to report, report them. Simply follow those rules as this version of sneaking and conniving is not cheating. It is simply finding a better way to educate children.

A note to educators, as we change to a new worldview of education, we must keep a strong focus on children's educational progress. As evidenced in a future chapter, you will be held accountable. This is not an excuse to go back to the good old days when students of privilege had advantage and learning was at random.

This is a call for teachers to step up to the plate, take responsibility, and work harder than you have ever worked before. Take pride in your profession and show what you can really do for children. The question then becomes are you willing to sneak and connive for kids, or sell them to the politicians?

What is significant is that all of these activities have a ton of reading and math built into them. Every activity is chock full of those skills in the student's educational plan and every minute of every activity is meaningful to enhance the child's future.

Infiltrating the system is a clandestine activity that can be easily accomplished under the current system and philosophy of education. These activities can be embedded and infused into the current curriculum, and only the children and parents will know the difference.

To continue to prepare the whole child for the future, our secret curriculum must be expanded well past the fundamentals isolated to the tradition of the testable. In this day and age of social media, we must address the everyday skills needed to ascend the social stratum to gain success. We must teach the whole child.

*"Educating our children is not just about imposing a body of knowledge on them. Rather, it involves preparing children from the early years for the world in which they will come of age. It means instilling a love of lifelong learning, creativity, self-expression and an appreciation for diversity." —Queen Rania of Jordan*

*Chapter 5*

# Developing Character in a Dangerous World

As we continue to build a school philosophy we must consider the skills needed to survive in a more intensified social world. A world that requires young people to develop the ability to survive against an onslaught of challenges to their everyday life. A world where social media scrutinizes every word with the potential to lead to new friendships or extreme violence depending on the direction it takes.

We may no longer ignore the necessity for character development as part of the curriculum. This is an area where we can build in a wide range of academics while focusing on the need for teaching the whole child.

## PROACTIVE CHARACTER DEVELOPMENT

Having good manners is of great importance to the well-being of each student. People with a good cadre of character skills tend to lead more productive and satisfying personal and interpersonal life. Here character development is taught using a structured format.

The teaching time frame for a character development session will vary from half an hour to introduce the skill to approximately forty-five minutes to present a scene. The components are modeling, role playing, performance feedback, and transfer of training. Many of these skills relate directly to the effort to abolish hate speech, bullying, and disruptive behavior in schools while reinforcing professionalism that is so important to future employment. Add a little creativity to this strategy and a unique lesson plan is developed. Give students ownership and their leadership will be surprising. Students will relish the "joy of learning." Here is an example of a weekly lesson plan to teach the skill of "Using Self Control."

Monday

- Introduce the skill and discuss it with the students.
- Ask students what the character trait means to them and chart the answers.
- Why might it be important to know how to use this skill?
- Brainstorm when one could use this skill.
- Have students use their notebooks and write the four steps in it as the teacher presents them.
- Leave the four steps where visible all week.

Steps

1. Tune in to what is going on in your body that may help you know that you are about to lose control of yourself.
   a. Are you getting: tense, angry, hot, or fidgety?
2. Decide what happened to make you feel this way.
   a. Consider outside events or actions that affected you
   b. Internal events such as thoughts may persist leading to potential actions.
3. Think about ways in which you might control yourself.
   a. Slow down
   b. Count to ten
   c. Assert yourself
   d. Leave the area
   e. What others can you think of?
4. Choose the best way for you to control yourself and do it.

Tuesday

- Highlight the key words in the steps . . . Tune, Decide, Think, Choose, . . . and talk about what they mean.
- Present a prepared activity using modeling; the teacher and a chosen student prepare a scene that takes place in a classroom.
  ○ The scene: The main actor controls yelling at teacher when the teacher criticizes them harshly.
- Students observe and critique the situation.
  ○ The next scene is in the home: The main actor controls self when a parent forbids the desired activity.
  ○ Students observe and critique the situation.
  ○ Third scene is with a peer group: The main actor controls self when a friend takes something without asking permission.
  ○ Students observe and critique and then discuss the importance of "Using Self Control."

Wednesday

- Students use 3"×5" cards on which to write a role-play situation. They set the scene, select the actors, and prepare a situation in which to use self-control.
  - The teacher asks for volunteers to demonstrate a role-play for the class.
  - The author of the situation chooses the actors, sets the stage, and directs the role-play.
  - When the role-play is finished, the students/observers critique the role-play and give feedback to the performers.
  - The teacher explains how to provide social reinforcement via praise, approval, and encouragement.
  - The teacher collects the student-written role-play cards.

Thursday

- Role-Play Day.
  - The role-play cards can be distributed randomly or chosen by students.
  - Small groups are formed, and students decide how to present the role-play. A variety of methods can be used for these presentations.
  - Students can give performance feedback via oral discussions or use of a written form. Students can critique themselves also.
  - The students can monitor the role-plays and point out the steps of the skill as the players demonstrate it.
  - Role-plays can be enhanced into vignettes. They can be audio or video recorded.

Friday

- Transfer of training can be discussed.
  - When would this skill be used?
  - How could it be generalized into the community? At home? On the job?
  - The Character Skill Homework Sheet is distributed and is to be taken home as a home project.
  - Parent is requested to role-play at home or in the community with their child. A situation is provided for the parent.
  - When completed, the homework sheet is to be returned to the teacher.
  - If possible, a transfer of training activity could be arranged. Example: Take students outside to play a game such as basketball, kickball, or capture the flag and monitor the use of this skill.
  - Students can critique themselves as to how they used the skill of "Using Self Control."

Students can also turn the tables and teach the adults a few character skills. What an interesting concept. It is important for adults in the school to model every one of the skills taught.

## Teachers Guide to the Skill of the Week

Here are some thoughts giving teachers direction in implementing a character-building program:

Objective: Provide skill building to enable students to address issues and adversity and then cope with personal and character problems that, at times, result in disruptive behaviors in and out of the school building.

Each week, a new character skill is taught in all classes and generalized throughout the school settings and at home.

- Character skills assessment is given to students and staff.
- Skills that are needed are documented and placed in a calendar.
- Steps to teach the skill are distributed and taught to the staff.
- Teacher presents the "Character Skill of the Week" using a specific model.
- The "Character Skill of the Week" is posted on school walls.
- The "Character Skill of the Week" sheet, with steps and the evaluation sheet is sent home every Friday.
- Students observed "using the skill" could be rewarded using various methods.
- The student is to return the parent evaluation sheet on Monday of the next week.

A character skills self-assessment taken by students could answer questions like these:

- Do I know of different ways to avoid fights?
- Is it easy for me to make the right choices?
- Do I get upset when I lose at a game?

Once the needed skills are defined, the calendar is created, and the character development lessons are organized.

## Manners Matter

In Milwaukee, Wisconsin's Bell Middle School, a program was developed called M&M RAP; Manners Matter, Respect All People. A small group was formed to lead the effort. They started by selecting a "skill of the week" designed to reinforce good behaviors. The students then develop a rap around that skill and presented it to other members of the group. This rap could also be used in the morning announcements to develop awareness for all students.

The students in the group would then pass out M&M RAP cards to those students they observed exhibiting that particular skill. A drawing was then held, and a prize awarded to the card chosen. In addition, that team of students would use a video camera to catch people using the skill of the week. This was especially interesting when they decided to use the cameras on teachers. It is so important for all adults to be good role models.

With this small group of students in the lead, a wide range of speakers were invited to present related views to the student body. To fully develop good work habits these students were "turned loose" to choose the speakers, contact them, and invite them to speak. They would also formally introduce them to the student body. Every opportunity is made available for students to practice skills necessary for their future. The lead group was rotated to allow many students to have this experience.

## STOP AND THINK BEFORE YOU ACT

### Staying Safe

Keeping student's safe is essential to maintaining an environment conducive to learning whether our attention is given to words that incite violence or the dangers prevalent in the world that sneak through the schoolhouse door to inflict damage on unsuspecting children.

Often violence begins with words, ill-used, that lead to fear by those at whom the words are directed. Hidden behind the fake exclusion of political correctness, hate speech, and bad manners that lead to violence are thriving. An environment conducive to learning must be free of those fears.

*Educators must be forever vigilant, prepared to confront issues that provoke fear promptly*

Everything from bullying to threats of violence, to mean spirited whispers, to physical contact must be addressed post haste. Never, ever should these concerns be ignored, pretending they will go away. They will not go away; they will lurk in the minds of the victims forever and must be confronted immediately. If bringing back political correctness is bringing back manners, so be it.

Of significance is that when a hate incident happens, it must be addressed not only with the students involved, but also with every student in the school to be taught as a lesson. When an incident happens in school, the word will spread rapidly. Administrative silence subtly condones those actions that can be so damaging to children. The bottom line however, lies in the classroom. Silence is not an option. After every hate incident, no matter how small, a discussion must begin in the classroom to take advantage of it as a teachable moment.

Critical thinking is again in the forefront. It is important to remind students that their words have consequences. Often children, especially in the middle years, will act without thinking deeply about what they say compared to what they feel. How will their words and actions affect others and how will they affect relationships with their peers? Harsh words, said without thinking, often lead to violence.

## PROTECTING THE SOUL OF CHILDREN

Encouraging signs are from a wide range of individuals and groups who are beginning to fight back. "School Racism, Sexism and Homophobia" is a group on Facebook dedicated to putting a focus on those very dangerous issues. They might easily include Xenophobia in the mix. College signs painted with swastikas, a black mannequin found hanging at a school and students chanting "build the wall" at a volleyball game are all incidents brought to the forefront by that Facebook group and many others.

Educators throughout the country are beginning to take action. "Right after the election, we started seeing people inside and outside of the classroom feeling emboldened to say racially charged things to many of our students" said Ryan Kaiser, Maryland´s teacher of the year in a Washington Post article. "That really started galvanizing how quickly we needed to get something done." Forty-four teachers who are all state "teachers of the year" have posted a video on their website, to speak out against bullying which is on the increase.

Teacher of the year Nate Bowling, in the same article stated, "This isn't a political thing, to say that students should be safe in our buildings. There's nothing political to me that our public schools are institutions of our democracy and should be protected." It is past time for educators within the schools to take action in the form of the everyday curriculum. It is essential that the schools and the children in them be kept safe always. The climate in this country is ripe for attacks on those of various ethnic cultures and that is playing out on a regular basis.

### Tackling Concerns Head On

Lately we have been overwhelmed with hate speech of all kinds from every direction imaginable. Of course, white supremacists have always had their say but that was kept to a minimum. Public opinion pushed hate speech and disrespect into the closet. The same could be said with Xenophobia, gender discrimination, and other issues as well. The language was hovering around the closet when it burst into the open by the overt actions of those in the public eye. How do we protect our children from these politicians who have such little regard for them?

An article entitled "Talking Race, Controversy, and Trauma" by Leah Shafer (February 21, 2017) from Usable Knowledge, Connecting Research to Practice by the Harvard Graduate School of Education had former teacher and school administrator Aaliyah El-Amin, making suggestions on how teachers can help students process traumatic events.

- Acknowledge traumatic events or circumstances. Bring up news with students the day after it breaks, even if details or consequences are still uncertain.
- Process and name emotions together. Help students identify their emotions through discussion circles or individual writing prompts. Describe your own emotions, whether they be outrage, fear, numbness, or uncertainty.
- Ask students what they know and what they need. Some students may have a thorough grasp of what's going on, but little idea of how it could impact them.
- Others may feel very affected, but, lack a nuanced understanding of the details.
- Open the discussion to figure out what students want to know, and, let them ask questions.
- Teach relevant information. Where possible, integrate current events into lesson plans to explain to students what's happened. Draw connections among the various forces facing communities of color. If you're unclear about details, be honest with your students, and work to investigate the details together.
- Connect students to resources. Show all students, including those who may be affected by new policies or rhetoric, that their school and teachers are there to help. Connect vulnerable students with local lawyers, social workers, and advocates who can provide them with the assistance they need.

No longer may we pretend problems don't exist when they are thrown into the faces of students. Students are more aware of these activities than they show. Regardless of appearances, students are often suffering deeply inside. The time for action is now.

## Hate Speech, a Community As Well As a Family Concern

Often schools are blamed for incidents that come in from the community or the home. Of course schools must respond to these incidents, but the responsibility does not lie solely with them. To thoroughly understand the problem there must be collaboration among all those concerned. They all share the responsibility to do their part. Community members, parents, and school personnel must team together to resolve all issues.

Quite often hate speech comes blurting out of a teenager's mouth. Taking the project into the home helps the student and the family by giving them some thoughts as to how to control their actions. Character development can be broken down into the following steps. Parents are asked to discuss these concerns with their child and, if possible role-play situations at home.

1. Understand how you feel when you are about to lose control of yourself.
2. What happened to make you feel this way?
3. What are the best ways to control yourself?
4. Choose the best way to control yourself, and, do it.

Here is an example of role playing at home:

- You control yourself when you are denied permission to go to the late movie on a school night.
  - Please describe how your son/daughter did while using the character skill in either the role-play or real life.
  - Encourage and praise your child when you see the skill appropriately used.
  - Remind him/her to use the character skill when necessary.

The teaching of character skills is not the single cure to the problems facing the youth of today. It is just one small piece of the puzzle. At the very least, it will be a reminder to the student to approach problems in a positive way. At the very most, students will use the skills that are taught.

A major step regarding a hate issue is to follow up with a community meeting allowing parents to share their thoughts about the issues at hand. This could be uncomfortable, but it is essential. The time to put our head in the sand is over. Community gatherings must happen on a continuous basis. The response, however, must have a positive tone and it must begin in the community immediately. Waiting to react would be too late to stop the damage. This is one bell we can't un-ring, but we can support good manners moving forward.

In urban areas, the issues will rise to the surface immediately. However, in many small rural communities that lack diversity, the issues are still often ignored. It is much easier to subtly ignore the problem hoping it will go away. In a small community in North Carolina, a hate incident happened in the local high school. A student was carrying a cross with the effigy of two black people hanging from nooses. The student left a classroom and went to other areas of the school where the student was stopped and disciplined.

The local NAACP got involved and agreed to work with the school at a later date. They held an excellent community meeting one year later, but the school basically swept it under the rug. The point is that a sense of urgency did not exist.

It is essential that a community meeting make everyone as comfortable as possible. Solutions come from a civil discussion, sharing ideas to come to resolution. Finger pointing and blaming resolves nothing. Many people have been entrenched in their beliefs and fears for years. They must be nudged away from their concerns with a belief that all people must be treated with respect. It is also very possible that many do not share the fears as they are reluctant to speak out to not offend those who do. Gatherings that are safe and comfortable for all will allow for a true exchange of ideas.

## BUILDING THE BUNKER OF SAFETY

Building a bunker of safety around our children does not mean isolate them to make them safe but broaden their views and expand this bunker around the community to better understand the issues confronting them in their future. The education curriculum must be extended beyond the narrow scope of testing to the vision of how things are seen from the perspective of neighbors and friends. Bring in community members and go out into the community to get a real view of the world.

### Safe Passage

When students feel safe, they are less likely to act out. Of primary concern in keeping students comfortable is to provide an environment conducive to learning. Neighborhood schools are ideal to enhance community building. Parents are near and are more likely to become full partners, local businesses are nearby and can aid the educational process and children can walk to school. They don't have to spend hours on the bus that can be otherwise spent in a variety of educational activities. The down side is, of course, the safety issue when on the journey from home to school.

*Is any neighborhood completely safe for children who walk to school?*

We never know what is lurking in the shadows on the walk home even in areas that are perceived as untouched by crime. Of course, we also never know what trouble a child can get into riding a bus with only a driver to supervise. Putting our focus on the path home, an effort must be made to assure safe passage for every student.

Of course, young children must have transportation as they would be less able to respond to a dangerous situation. But what about the middle years or secondary school student, how do they get home safely without running into problems or creating the problems themselves?

The development of "Safe Paths" is one step in the right direction.

- Put a map of the neighborhood on the wall.
- Add pin marks for every home student will be walking to.
- Locate the major streets that will take the students close to their homes.
- Connect with parents as well as other neighbors along that route to be aware of school start up and closing times.
- Ask those parents to step out on their front porch to keep an eye out for the students.
- Be sure parents have contact information for the school.
- In more dangerous areas assign a staff member to patrol the areas in a car.
- Contact every business along the way to have them look out for the kids.
- Stay vigilant until every child is home.

This doesn't solve every problem but it does increase the safety of all students.

> *When children are dismissed from school, have a staff member or administrator get in their car and drive the "safe paths" to assure no students are harmed.*

## Approaching a Crisis

Keeping the school environment safe is critical to the mental health of the students. Educators throughout the years have been prepared for any possible situation that may arise. We knew the severest of problems could occur on a regular basis. A school staff must become adept at handling any situation in a professional manner be they in the school or on the safe path home.

It is important to approach crisis situations in a manner that does not allow for injury or harm to anyone. To accomplish this, the Crisis Prevention Institute (www.crisisprevention.com) is designed to prepare educators for any situation including those involving out of control students. The information proves useful to the students as well, as they can learn how to better handle crisis situations.

To begin we must focus on the initial approach to a person whose actions are perceived as problematic. This is especially relevant in the school setting as no one ever knows when a serious problem will arise. So how do we approach a situation like this without allowing it to escalate?

We must first understand that we have no idea what is inside the mind of the person we are confronting. A child who has been severely abused, for example, will be numb to any threats of punishment that we offer. There is nothing that can scare them. A child who is on drugs might very well be incoherent and not able to respond to the threat of punishment. The child we are approaching might have no affliction, but the reality is we won't know that. We then assume the worst and hope for the best.

Following the guidelines of nonviolent crisis intervention, the first step is to be supportive. To give the perception as well as the reality of being supportive, it is important to relate to your students. Without that connection, the chances of escalation increase. A teacher or administrator, connected to the student, has a much better chance of de-escalating the situation simply by talking it through.

An example of what works is to approach the person of concern in a non-threatening manner. The Crisis Prevention Institute (CPI) teaches how and where to stand to achieve this end. The conversation that follows must be aimed at de-escalating a potential crisis. After confidence is gained one might say "We need you to move out of the hall to a quieter room, ok?" Be patient but persistent and then walk the person to the alternate location. Do not be in a hurry.

Depending on the intensity of the situation, this might take a while. If the situation intensifies, other designated staff members may be there as soon as possible. The first staff member on the scene, however, is the only one to do the talking. If the student focuses their anger on the first responder, that staff member then steps back out of sight and allows another to defuse the situation.

Often this will deescalate the situation. If not, there is more than one person to become forceful if necessary. Even if the incident was a minor shouting match this approach will not leave anyone dead and will come to an eventual solution.

There are those who see this approach as weak, however, it, is more accurate to call it humanizing. When we look past the outer shell into the inner soul we see a human being. That's the inner person we are trying to reach because that is the person who will give a rational response.

However, if at any time the process isn't working proceed to step two, directive. That is when the staff member takes charge of the situation. This is when a second responder must be nearby. Anything to avoid handling the situation alone is good. First you have an additional set of eyes, and second the other staff member can step in to mediate if necessary.

The second responder is of utmost importance if a restraint is necessary. A restraint should only be used when absolutely necessary like breaking up a fight, a student with a weapon, or an out of control student, and only when every other option has been tried. At CPI training, we were taught never to restrain someone alone. It is not safe. We were taught how to control someone physically without hurting them or us. And never, ever would we put hands on or even near the throat.

Once under control, they would be held in silence until one person will ask if they are ready to cooperate. No restraints should ever be made without the proper training and only when the safety of others is at stake. The CPI is a great resource to deal with crisis situations in the school. They would also be valuable for the training of community resources such as police departments and mental health facilities.

It is the hope that these techniques will never be used. However, to assure everyone is ready, all school personnel should receive this preparation. This even works in a simple argument situation that will probably never lead to a crisis. It just makes the school atmosphere better in the long run.

## Securing the Building

It is important to understand that although the building must be secure, it must also provide a welcoming environment. In order to secure a building, it is not necessary to turn it into a prison like atmosphere. Cameras and a buzzer system can allow swift access to the building with minimal interference with the daily routine. Every effort must be made to assure a positive atmosphere once in the building. Security can be provided without diminishing a welcoming atmosphere. Large plants placed around the hallways enhanced the comfort while murals on the walls, a result of our art class, not only were beautiful but made a statement.

Starting a school with a Community Aide in lieu of a safety aide enhanced the atmosphere as they did not wear uniforms. This Community Aide was available to connect with parents both in the parent center within the school and in their living rooms. At a time when a student caused difficulties the Community Aide could walk the student to their home to have a discussion with their parent. Teachers were able to contact parents both by phone and by visiting the home. As our teachers were grouped in teams of four adults, three could cover the classes while the fourth could visit a home. Flexibility was the key.

Building security is of utmost importance in providing for the school as a safe house. Begin with a security check that assesses every possible means of entry for someone intent on doing harm. Every possible entrance to the building must either be locked or covered by a staff member. Cameras are an asset and do not interfere with the welcoming atmosphere of the building.

A check around the doors should show that there are no adjacent windows that can be broken to allow access to a door handle and easy entry.

When adjacent windows are a problem, security is easily provided through a door handle guard. This simple hardware change could make the difference between life and death.

In addition to securing the building, a check of the perimeter must be ongoing. It is much better to observe potential problems as they approach the building rather than after. In severe cases, that gives police a head-start on dealing with the problem and school administrators a chance to "lock down" the school. In potentially less severe cases, it gives the school community aide or teachers in charge a chance to meet the problem outside the school long before a disruption to students occur.

There are many ways to secure the perimeter of the building. Various options including cameras or personal surveillance would also be valuable, not only to the school but to the immediate community. More "eyes" in the community equals less problematic activity. A hotline for neighborhood parents along with a coordinated call system would be un-intrusive but valuable when neighborhood concerns existed.

All children must feel safe in their school knowing that every entrance is secured, every potential violent act is dealt with and every educator is alert to assure the comfort and safety of every student. There are no short cuts when it comes to the safety of every child. No school, wherever it is, is exempt. The teachers, parents, children, and community must know that the school is the ultimate safe house.

Security begins at the front door with every policy rigidly enforced. We want to assure all visitors that they are welcome to the school; at the same time, we must assure no dangerous individuals are allowed to enter. There are some simple steps that can stop trouble at the front door:

- Everyone entering the building must be welcomed by a staff member and escorted to the office to check in.
- Everyone must receive a pass that is visible, to go to their designated location. This pass may be enhanced to reflect the welcoming atmosphere of the school. Student art work is one suggestion.
- The teacher in the classroom to be visited must be contacted prior to the visitor leaving the office.
- Schools should consider metal detectors if deemed necessary.
- An emergency buzzer may be considered for every classroom to alert administration to the need for assistance.

Although this seems cumbersome, the process will take only a minute or two and all will feel safe and visitors will feel welcome at the same time.

## School Response Saves Lives

A plan of action is necessary for the safety of all. Communications with local police departments must focus on a continuous update of the needs of the safety of the school. When a major problem occurs within the building, a lock down policy must be in place to deal with it. All staff must know what they are going to do to protect the safety of the children.

This begins with a signal from the administrator. It is often best to have a code word that can be announced over the public-address system signaling teachers to act without causing students to panic. One example is "attention teachers; Mr. Jones is in the building."

Every teacher will have an assignment. Those with classes will shut and lock the doors. Others will have assignments to go to specific checkpoints to assure all outside doors are locked, the hallways are cleared, or prepare a staging area for police and as a communication center. An office staff as well as one more designated staff member will be assigned to call police.

As the problem progresses, further directions would be given. In the case of shots fired in the building, an additional signal will notify teachers. Following the incident, a room will be made available to meet with the press and make calls to parents. If the building is made safe, parents would be able to come to that area to pick up their children. A neighborhood building within walking distance will be available if students must leave the building.

Although this may sound harsh to those who live in areas perceived to be safe, simply remember, mental health issues can happen anywhere. Hate is spreading like wildfire to every corner of the world and those who are on the edge are the most vulnerable. And when properly implemented, these actions would be unnoticed by the casual observer.

## Maintaining Vigilance

Every school shooting, even when there are no injuries or deaths, are traumatic to students. According to the United States Center for Disease Control, "Not all injuries are visible. Exposure to youth violence and school violence can lead to a wide array of negative health behaviors and outcomes, including alcohol and drug use, and suicide. Depression, anxiety, and many other psychological problems, including fear, can result from school violence." This is a major health concern for all young people. The problem is evident but what is the solution?

Teachers must always be vigilant no matter how safe the school seems to be. Utilizing professionals in psychology, they must be trained to recognize danger signs in the action of students. These signs must never be ignored. Although it is important not to over react, it is as important to make teachers and support staff aware of the slightest signs of problems. Remember, with 81 percent of school shooters, someone had information that the shootings might happen. In addition, parents and neighbors could attend training sessions that allow them to see "red flags" when they occur.

It is important for a team of educators and police officers to form a committee to devise security related policies in the school. A referral process for potential offenders must then be activated. Upon activation, a wide variety of responses would be implemented. Everything from simple school counseling to a psychiatric referral must be on the table. Teaming with parents and community members will assure a better chance to prevent a crisis from happening.

The most noticeable warning signs include students displaying social problems, especially social isolation. For adolescents, being a part of a social group, no matter how small, is extremely important. Those who deliberately choose not to be a part of the group may need help.

According to www.skylandtrail.org, "another warning sign is thoughts or actions focused on violence. Expressing violent fantasies or engaging in acts of aggression toward animals may indicate a problem." Finally, a change in behaviors and performance in schools is another indicator. The school psychologist would be able to provide more detailed information and must be consulted on a regular basis.

Do not let any of these concerns pass you by. Respond accordingly before it is too late. As for students, if you see something, say something. Word of mouth works best. Also, if you see someone who needs a friend, be a friend. Lives might be saved.

Mental health and drug and alcohol involvement go hand in hand. Those afflicted are more likely to be involved in gun violence. Alcoholism is a family disease. It affects everyone in the family in one way or another. Those who have the disease have a tough road to beating it, while those family members who are left to deal with it on an everyday basis have tremendous emotional stress.

This disease is one that may not be allowed to persevere in schools or anywhere else. It is easy to believe the alcoholic can stop drinking whenever they want, but that is simply not the case. Although not curable, an alcoholic can be in recovery. The beginning of that process is when an educator recognizes the problem.

According to Indiana University of Pennsylvania, Alcohol, Tobacco and other Drugs program, these may be signs of addiction;

- Appearing under the influence in class.
- Smelling of alcohol during the day.
- Missed coursework or classes due to alcohol or drug use.

- Preoccupation with alcohol and other drug use, which may be evident in conversation or course papers.
- Changes in academic performance.
- Changes in mood or behavior.
- Getting into fights or becoming aggressive while under the influence.
- Inability to control drinking; drinking more than intended; inability to have just one or two drinks.
- Increase in tolerance to alcohol use.
- Trouble with police or school officials because of alcohol or drug use.
- Expressed concern from others because of the usage.
- Blackouts (loss of memory) from alcohol or drug use.
- Drinking or drug use as a main priority.

As for intervention, it is important not to let any inappropriate behaviors go unnoticed.

- Privately let the student know you are genuinely concerned.
- Describe to the student the specific behaviors that have caused you to be concerned.
- Speak to the student in an objective, unequivocal way.
- Have resource information available.
- Attempt to redirect the conversation when the student provides irrational excuses.
- Offer to assist the student in making the contact with the appropriate program that deals with alcohol and/or drug abuse.

There are many ways to do damage to children during their tender K-12 school years. Remember, as an educator, you are the one who can make the difference. Whether it is protecting their souls from the spoken evils in today's world or from the dangers that lurk around every corner, nothing should be ignored.

Although there are many irrational fears, a strong, well thought out safety plan must be in place for those fears that may become real. For success, there must be a multifaceted approach. Not only does the issue of protecting children include school security and the strengthening of mental health programs, but also there must be an effort to assure every fool doesn't have a gun!

*We must listen to the wise words from the students at Marjory Stoneman Douglas High School in Parkland, Florida as no one knows better than those who were directly affected.*

*Chapter 6*

# A Force to Be Reckoned With

As we embed and infuse great ideas into our curriculum, we must face the reality that it is the system and philosophy of education that is broken. To resolve this issue will take more than a band aid approach. It has taken hundreds of years to develop this entrenched system and it will be no small task to change it. Teachers will not be able to do it alone; they must seek out agents of kindred minds to take on the challenge.

The system and philosophy of education is stuck in an era where children are shackled by the ways of the past, forced into educational confinement, being controlled by those who are driven by their own power, ego, and control. There is a cycle of control beginning with corporations who own the politicians who control the schools who then control the minds of the students away from critical and rational thinking.

To break this cycle, systemic change must begin from the ground up. There is now an urgency to empower children to chase their dreams, parents to become full partners in the process, and educators to take back their profession. The ultimate goal is to protect students from those who simply want them to be obedient workers. That's not what innovative businesses want, that's not what is necessary to make communities thrive. However, throughout history, that has been the fundamental purpose of education. Change will not be easy. The whole paradigm of thought must change. The implementers must act as a cohesive team and have total commitment to forge ahead with this concept.

*"If 90% of the people don't pooh pooh you, you don't have a great idea."* —Ted Turner

# SECURE OUR STRONGEST PARTNERS, THE PARENTS

We begin by preparing the ground work to quash a broken system of education and design a new one that truly does respect the intelligence and abilities of all children. To reach this goal, parents must be empowered as the child's first and foremost teacher as well as a full partner and adviser to the school.

This philosophy opens a new world for parents. It is always a struggle for them to try to assure a school is doing what is best for their child. Is their child learning anything, are they safe, are teachers sensitive to their needs? Issues are many as more and more parents voice their concerns about quality education.

This new plan must be designed to resolve the problems that concern parents about their schools through systemic change. To accomplish this, parents must be involved from conception, as full partners. Parents, as the guiding lights of a school designed for children, must no longer take a back seat in the educational direction of the school. Their views must be acknowledged every step along the way. With a strong partnership, an innovative plan will be developed that can better meet the needs of their children. But this partnership must be real. The parent role must be meaningful.

Too often, parental involvement is a facade, only giving the impression of real involvement. Often parent "councils" have the few available parents appearing to represent all parents, with minimal or no contact with the majority of the parents. Some schools require their governance boards be made up of 51 percent parents, allowing them to brag about their parental involvement. While these parents hold more votes than other group members, they rarely represent anyone but themselves or, in some cases, are simply a puppet of the school administration. Parent groups often become superficial, as their input is only solicited on non-educational issues like fundraisers or prom decorations.

Parental involvement on an all-school level must become real. School personnel must seek out parental advice in meaningful ways such as giving direction to student goals and proficiencies as well as to the curriculum and school design. The effectiveness of utilizing parent input is one indicator of a successful school.

It is essential, under this new plan, to keep parents in the forefront of their child's education. They must take their rightful place on the school Empowerment Council. The fundamental philosophy must open doors to assure involvement at the core level of the school. Here is our promise to parents:

- Rather than being deceived by artificial letter grades, parents will be told exactly what their child has learned based on clear documentation.
- With parent involvement in their students educational planning, there will be transparency as to what their child will learn.
- Every parent will be recognized and contacted on a regular basis with a wide range of information about the school.
- Every parent will provide their thoughts on major issues concerning the school. The school personnel will then respond as to the action taken on those issues.
- Parent evaluation of the school will be included as a formal part of the school assessment.
- Easy access to the school will allow parents to observe their children in action. They are welcome to join their children in the classroom as well as on community experiences and all other activities.

When we say, "parents are welcome," we mean it. The classroom, as well as the extended classroom in the community, must be a friendly place for parents. Welcomed to witness first hand everyday events, parents are encouraged to volunteer in the classroom. A school's need for chaperones drives volunteerism in most schools, but our philosophy is to throw open the doors to involve parents at any time throughout the year.

## Garnering the Support of Families

A plan to embrace the support and guidance of parents is put into place on the first day of school. They are welcomed into the school as full partners recognizing that no one knows their children better than they do. Here's how we begin the year:

- Prior to the beginning of the school year, plan a family meeting at the school to update all parents on the new school year and explain the school philosophy.
- Set up a Parent Empowerment Counsel with a wide diversity of representation. Explain how this counsel operates and how surveys will include all parents to receive full input.
- Create a calendar for meetings at times that are more likely to meet family time frames.
- Make it easy for parents to participate in meetings by serving a small meal. This may seem trivial but it is difficult for parents to combine work, cooking, as well as attending meetings. Catered meals, barbecues,

and student-prepared meals are excellent ways to encourage participation. And siblings are invited. Food is the Great Uniter!

Parent surveys are essential to the gathering of information that is meaningful. To assure all parents have access to the survey, send someone into every home. That will be impossible and very expensive you might think. Not if you get creative. What if that "someone" is their child? The best way to record parents' thoughts on crucial issues is through open and honest surveys that utilize the interview. To accomplish this, students are taught to gather information using a variety of methods. They then plan how to compile and use that information.

Training students to conduct surveys would not only be a great way to connect with the parents but will also be an educational experience.

Objective: Students will be able to gather information by using a survey.

• Decide what information needs to be gathered.
• Teach students how to interview using role-play procedures.
• Visit a mall or other locations to gain information from those doing consumer surveys.
• Teach students how to gain facts using a library, the internet, and other resources.
• Teach students how to use a survey to gain information.
• Decide how to compile and report the information gathered.
• Complete a final product.

Designing and administering surveys is a great skill for students to develop, and they can use their parents as practice while gathering important information at the same time. Students would ensure that all parent voices are heard.

It is important that information gathered is no longer filed away, never again to be seen. The results of the information gathered, as well as the manner to which it will be used, are reported to parents. This is not just a stunt designed to give the appearance of parental involvement, this is parental involvement.

As parents become fully immersed in the school philosophy, they then become agents in the community, advocating for the high-quality innovation that has been implemented in their school. Remember, they have been full partners from the beginning. Now they become a powerful force in supporting their school's innovation. There will be attempts by the agenda driven politicians to silence them, but parents must be relentless in their effort.

Implementing a new system and philosophy of education is extremely difficult. It is important to the process that parents are aware of the changes made every step of the way. All ideas must be on the table for parents to see awaiting their response. It is the job of the innovative team to sell those ideas that will support children and the job of parents to present those ideas to the community at large.

# THE AGENDA OF CHILDREN

## Looking to the Leaders

Essential to systemic change is the drawing together of teachers and parents of kindred minds. Bringing parent organizations into the mix is essential. Not only must they be involved on the local level, it is imperative that they are active throughout the nation organizations like The Parent Teacher Association, Parent Teacher Organizations, Parents Around America, and Class Size Matters are a few that are essential support systems for parents.

Seek out innovators in the field of education to be on your Empowerment Council. You not only would benefit from the input these leaders will bring, but choose those who will contribute to the school in future years. As you consider your community, you will see educators, parents, and community members that support the agenda of children.

Looking around the country, there are great examples of people who exemplify the teaching profession. Educators like: Dr. LaShawn Roscoe Clark, a teacher from Illinois who was able to stay one step ahead of her rambunctious students and take them into the community; Rita Solnet, from Florida who stands with Parents Across America for educational justice; Ranjit Singh, a teacher in Wisconsin who has a phenomenal connection to every last one of her students; Mr. Lonnie Anderson, an administrator in Wisconsin, who has so many creative ideas, Dr. Angela Dye, an innovative educator and author from Georgia who has demonstrated, in the trenches, that innovation not only can work, but must work and Seno Luz Estela Narvaez Lambrano, CEO of PROSEFAM school and foundation in Barranquilla Columbia who has implemented great innovative ideas for her students from their "pobre barrio." There are so many more waiting in the wings to develop the agenda of children.

More important, every leader in innovation must gather together supporters and have them serve on your Empowerment Council. Not only will they have input, they will be agents in place to promote the agenda of children.

*Now this is a force to be reckoned with!*

# LEADERS OF KINDRED MINDS

A perusal of the neighborhood will find many companies with influence who are dissatisfied with outcomes of the antiquated system of education. Selection must be a careful process designed to avoid bringing in the nay-sayers, but those of kindred mind must be located. Education is failing those businesses who want thinkers in their companies, not just those who are obedient.

It is necessary to vet all of those seeking to help as many may be artificial and destructive to your efforts.

The same effort goes for politicians, some of whom are not driven by artificial agendas. This vetting process is more difficult due to the nature of politics. However, good local politicians are easier to identify as they have friends and foes that you know and that you can trust. They can be a tremendous help if they are fully involved in the agenda of children as they can offset all of those who will demean your efforts based on their power, ego, and control.

Although the building process will be visible, efforts must be clandestine in nature as agenda driven politicians will fight you with every fiber of their being. If you are persistent and are for kids, you will win out in the end. Change is a slow process, but the table has been set with the efforts of organizations such as BATS, Parents Across America, and Network for Public Education. Now is the time to subvert the system, fighting quietly for the agenda of children. Once you pull together a team of kindred minds that truly understands education, and put parents and especially students in the lead, you have a force to be reckoned with.

## OVERHAULING A TARGET SCHOOL

Now that the team is in place, our propaganda machine must begin by working with parents to opt out from the huge standardized test. The difference however, is our propaganda will be based entirely on the truth.

Let the parents tell the truth about how worthless the test is to teachers and how it is used to artificially demean schools and rank and sort children for no apparent reason. Let them tell how the test comes to teachers too late to be effective rendering it meaningless for children. And then present a better idea because without a better idea, you too will be whistling into the wind.

Public relations must begin with a subtle approach as relatively few in the media thoroughly understand the fundamental needs of education. There is a powerful lobby for agenda driven politicians that have been bombarding the media with the only ideas many seem to understand. The rhetoric of school reform simply pits traditional public schools against charters, choice, and private schools to embolden their own power, ego, and control.

Again, referring to the "confirmation bias," journalists in need of headlines and sound bites find critical thinking too cumbersome. However, there have been those who have written stories about education. This occurs on a regular basis in *Education Week*, a weekly publication that specializes in innovative education issues. Their focus is solely on education allowing them to dig deeply into current issues.

If you look hard enough, you will find journalists who understand the need for change. The charge is to convince them that you are not simply ideologues but your reform will actually work. For that to happen, you must have a plan of action, in every last detail.

The reality is that the system and philosophy of education has not kept pace with the needs of the students. Considering the entire system is broken, it is difficult to find a wealth of information actively utilized in existing schools. However, you can refer to Montessori Schools who have similar concepts or the Mission Hill School founded by Deborah Meier or the Milwaukee Village School, developed by this author and Mary Gale Budzisz as described in the book *Quashing the Rhetoric of Reform*, a Rowman & Littlefield publication. Montessori has been around a long time; the Mission Hill School philosophy is reflected in the writings of Deborah Meier and the Village School was short lived but put into place many of these concepts and experienced enough to believe they would work.

The mold must be broken, and it must be broken from the bottom up. There is little chance that it will be broken from the top down as policies continue to be developed based on antiquated information and philosophies.


## IS STUMBLING AND BUMBLING A GOOD THING?

Hampered by the outdated history of education, the challenge becomes much larger as there are those who lack professional knowledge at the helm. Rarely will you find quality decision making at the highest levels as the rhetoric of reform trumps the real agenda of children. In the long list of goals spewed out by the agenda driven politicians, it is unlikely that innovation will be at the top of the list.

Change is slow but must be a steady process. Folk singer Pete Seeger talked about the folk process as songs develop with each musician that touches them. Remember, WD-40 had thirty-nine failures before they were finally successful. Now the question is, will we take the failures of the past and move forward or will we go back to the failed times of yore when education was designed to rake a few geniuses from the rubbish. Will the new "whole child" reform process be implemented or discarded and replaced by the rhetoric of reform?


### Remaining Vigilant

Educators must remain vigilant. Keep up the fight against standardized strategies that do damage to students. Keep up the fight against a competition system of education that bleeds the soul out of the losers. Keep up the fight against the slavery based system of education that keeps students off an even playing field, designed to keep a people down.

But, keep an eye out for the time when with trial and error and more error the nay-sayers stumble upon the way schools should be. Be prepared with your own assessment plan that truly measures the needs of students. Be prepared to provide every student with their pathway to success, not in lock step but as individual human beings.

As the Education Secretary implements her plan, be ready to implement your own clandestine system and philosophy of education. Education Secretaries, throughout history, have missed the mark. Guaranteed, they will continue to stumble and bumble but while they are trying to find their way, educators already know what must be done.

As politicians present simplistic solutions to complex problems, be prepared to activate your agents throughout your community to develop a new, innovative system and philosophy of education. Educators must raise their voices, regardless of the consequences, as they and they alone have the experience, education, and connection with children and their families to truly promote the agenda of children.

If politicians don't protect the children who need us the most, speak out and be heard. There are laws dating back to 1974 that protect the right of a free and appropriate education for children with special needs. Speak up for those rights and expand them for all children because all children are different.

If politicians try to eliminate unions, teachers must speak out and let the world know that you will not be silenced. Ask why would they want to silence teachers, those who are closest to the students and their families. Ask why children don't deserve a small class size to allow for differentiated learning. Remind them that children are not simply an extension of one child, but they are different, with different educational approaches necessary to serve them well.

If the politicians have a poor plan for accountability, tell them you are not afraid of accountability, you will measure up on all counts with an accountability system designed on an even playing field. And if politicians don't seem to be knowledgeable in the trends of education, let them stumble and bumble as long as you move ahead, from the ground up, to serve your children well. You become, not only the teacher of children, you become the teacher of educational leaders through your example. Together we will create an educational tsunami that cannot and will not be stopped. Once the dominoes start to fall there is no stopping them. Together with parents as partners, the agenda driven politicians will be neutered, unable to justify their artificial educational philosophies. There is no stopping the agenda of children.

## Together We Can Make Miracles Happen

As teachers in the trenches you must take the lead, as a partner with parents and students, to develop the kind of change necessary for the success of all children. It must be understood that most people want what's best for children. Most want the same thing for children, but few know how to accomplish that. Once the ideas begin to spread and take hold it is with utmost confidence that the old system will fall like dominoes replaced by the agenda of children.

At that point, it will make no difference if schools are traditional, charter, private, or any other structural design. Everyone will find their niche. Traditional public schools will lead the way serving the clear majority of children. Charters might go back to being University Schools for teacher training or alternative sites for those too old to attend in the traditional setting. Private religious schools will serve those with strong religious beliefs.

Once schools decide to collaborate rather than compete there is no limit to the quality of education children will receive. It is the heart and soul of teachers everywhere that can give children their best education. No one else can do it as teachers everywhere stand united for the agenda of children.

*Once teachers, parents, community leaders, vetted business leaders and others of kindred minds band together, they will be a force to be reckoned with.*

# Chapter 7

# Subverting the System

It is time to put on your trench coat, pull your Fedora over one eye and slither into the shadows because you are about to embark on a journey that is essential for the well-being of all children, more dangerous than 007 could imagine. You are about to team with parents and community members to subvert your school to offer children a high-quality education not only preparing them for critical thinking, not only preparing them for creativity but also preparing them to thrive in their community. The ultimate goal is to help students rise above the confirmation bias to educate the whole child and beyond. When dealing with politicians one must sneak and connive one's way to supporting the children who have been shackled for centuries.

Envision a school where all children have equal access to a quality education, taught in a way that is real, taken from "where they are" on their pathway to success at their best rate. Where learning opens doors to the dreams of every child, recognizing that no one will ever know where or when genius will unfold until it evolves.

Imagine a school where assessment is not cheapened by the narrow scope of the standardized test, but broadened to become a stepping stone for the whole child learning experience. A school where, as in life, learning is a constant flow of problem solving experiences driven by the reality that failure is not only an option but an integral tool, guiding students on their pathway to success. And where teachers have the freedom to innovate in the best interest of their students.

## THE CHAOS OF CHANGE

The time has come to become risk takers and change the system of education from the ground up, bending a few rules but recognizing that most rules are not rules at all, we just think they are. No one else is going to do it for children so teachers, the ones in the trenches, must.

The only ones standing in the way are the politicians and they can be deceived. To achieve this goal, teachers must continue to march and chant, filling the streets to bring awareness to the public of the crisis at hand. Their ulterior motive, however, will be to create a diversion while those in the trenches, sneak around in a clandestine manner and implement a system that serves children well.

To be fully prepared, we bring together our team of parents, teachers, and administrators of kindred minds, to develop an initial plan. A well scrutinized group of business representatives along with community advocates will bring a needed viewpoint to the team. You can bet there will be a wide range of Principals ready to jump on board. This team will develop specific questions designed to get at the basic problems of education.

Do letter grades tell parents and students what they have learned? Should children be pushed forward with a D- if they don't understand the material? What happens to children who are failed back to the beginning so often that when they turn twenty they are still in school? Will students, ready to move forward at a faster rate, continue to be held back simply because they are in a designated grade? Must children all have the same pathway to success?

There are many similar questions that get to the bottom of the problems in the educational structure. Once these questions are developed, the team is turned loose to ask every parent, teacher, and community member within hearing range, their views. That includes the parents who are disenfranchised, out there alone doing the best they can.

This will be the most difficult job imaginable. Change is chaotic at best, but with the powerful opposition of agenda driven politicians, it will be dangerous. The livelihood of teachers may be at stake but the salvation of children is imperative. To promote new innovative ideas, seek out those teachers who will challenge the thinking of the team as well as provide a service to the children once the ideas are implemented.

This is the beginning of a broad-based support system necessary to share ideas as well as to network the community for systemic change. Once the team is functioning, with input from all, they develop the resolve to reform the system and philosophy of education. They then take action!

*After we infiltrate the curriculum with creative ideas, we are now ready to take on the challenge of systemic change, and those in the trenches will lead. Fasten your seat belts because this will be a bumpy ride.*

# DESIGNING THE STUDENTS
# PATHWAY TO THEIR FUTURE

Charter, choice, traditional public and private schools are all in the same boat because they are all under the same artificial guidelines. It takes more than a name change to improve education. The artificial system of education that has been developed across the world throughout the centuries must no longer be supported. It is essential that a proficiency based system of education that promotes critical thinking through differentiated instruction and demonstrations of learning be implemented to make this mission successful.

Essential to a successful mission is to develop a proficiency system that does not strip the students of their culture. It is essential that students, as they develop through the years, choose the subject matter that enhances their passion for learning. Not everyone has the same interests so not everyone will take the same pathway. In addition, it must be assured that this system does not push students away from school simply because they don't learn as fast as our elitist desires demand.

A proficiency based system must be developed that does not depend on calling children smart or stupid, weak or strong, fast or slow, just to justify the egos of agenda driven politicians. This proficiency based system must recognize differences in students and develop their individual pathway to success.

*Once we embark upon change, the antiquated system and philosophy of education will tumble and fall like dominoes. There will be no turning back.*

The joy of learning is so important when we understand that children will memorize when we tell them only to be left with little knowledge. They will only learn when they are ready. They still control their minds and will open and close them based on *their perception* of the value of the incoming information. So, let the dominos fall!

## Developing the Map, Domino #1

Fundamental to a fair and just system of education is that each child has their own MAP (My Action Plan), as a guideline to their success. This MAP, domino number one, takes the form of a proficiency (or learning goal) checklist developed by educators at the local level with support from parents and students. This checklist is personal as it gives direction to the child's individual curriculum and therefore to daily projects but is also broad enough to include quality standards determined to be necessary for all students.

It is important to remember that their individual pathway might include subject matter that is unique to the student. As students complete this check list, they are cognizant of what they are learning and its value to their future. As each check has an authentic assessment attached to it, the learning becomes real to the student, empowering them to take charge of their educational lives.

> *"We actually checked off that piece of information learned (on the checklist) whenever it was completed. That way you don't get kids sliding through the cracks and failing later in life." —Chante Strehlke, former Milwaukee Village School student.*

Unique to this process, the student continuously moves forward through the checklist on an individual basis, never forced backward by an antiquated system of failure that has the ultimate effect of pushing students out of school. To maintain the positive effect of the process, grade levels are no longer indicators of achievement. That role becomes the domain of the proficiency checklist.

Here's a sketch of what a MAP might look like. The MAP, of course will be in much greater detail and may change as needed.

## The Map Outline

Communication Skills
  a. Reading
    i. ____ Identify and discuss the main theme of a written work.
    ii. ____ Be able to articulate the difference between fact, fantasy, and opinion.
  b. Writing
    i. ____ Identify incorrect punctuation in an article
    ii. ____ Write a resume using a proper format
  c. Speaking
    i. ____ Use acceptable pronunciation and enunciation when giving a speech
    ii. ____ Give an effective oral presentation
  d. Listening
    i. ____ Demonstrate attentive listening with immediate responses.
    ii. ____ Listen for main ideas in a spoken presentation or a musical presentation.
  e. Performing
    i. ____ Communicate a specific message through performing in an area of the arts of the students choosing
    ii. ____ Attend and analyze a performance of the student's interest

Problem Solving and Analytical Thinking
- a. Computing
  - i. \_\_\_\_ Convert decimals to fractions for the purpose of consumer understanding and demonstrated in a household budget.
  - ii. \_\_\_\_ Develop an engineering project using a wide range of mathematical skills.
- b. Measurement
  - i. \_\_\_\_ Build a model house to the exact dimensions of a real house.
  - ii. \_\_\_\_ Measure a floor for carpeting.

This is simply an outline of what a proficiency checklist might look like and how skills can be demonstrated and reported as opposed to a letter grade. The student's checklist, along with statements of their progress, will be more detailed and more specific to the student and their levels of performance. The progress report would include much more than just a checklist, it would include statements defining progress in detail to assure all children are monitored for their accomplishments. Letter grades will become obsolete.

Although many students will be on a similar level, others may not. Those not on the same level will move at their own pace. Surprisingly this can be done within the current system and philosophy of education. There are no rules against this style of innovation, just the pressure from agenda driven politicians who will fight it with every ounce of their being to maintain their power, ego, and control. Just don't tell them until it's too late and the plan has been fully implemented.

*The best part is these statements of learning completely replace letter grades which are gone forever.*

## Gaining Success by Failing, Domino #2

As we sabotage the outdated and destructive system of education we need to infiltrate the infrastructure to let the dominos fall in the way that benefits children. While domino number one, the proficiency checklist, drives the child's educational life, the second domino to fall is the outdated, destructive system of failure. The current system design assures many students will be pushed out of school. With every failure, they get further behind until they have no hope of graduating.

Remember WD-40? What does a lubricant have to do with failure? The name of the lubricant, WD-40 came from the thirty-nine failures they needed to eventually come up with success on the 40th try thus perfecting their water displacement product. What would have happened if they gave up after they failed the first few times? The product would have never gained success.

Under this new system of education, when failing an authentic proficiency assessment, students will be able to re-take it when they are ready. They will fail as many times as necessary to get it right.

No hard and fast failure, no moving on with a D-, but a failure for learning where students can again have high expectations without being pushed into the black hole and forgotten. The brains of many politicians are ingrained to believe that if failure does not include "a pound of flesh," children will never learn. "Children must be taught a lesson." When asked why students don't fail in this system, the response is that there is more failure in this system than in the previous one. Students simply learn from it and move on, the way we do in life.

Here's a story about Captain Dave "Full Ahead" Kennedy as told by singer songwriter Gordon Bok. Captain Kennedy was a pilot of an ocean-going vessel that measured two football fields in length. Bok stated that Kennedy could read the mind of that ship and gently bring it into port without a hitch. But he didn't get that way by doing everything right. Quite the contrary. He learned by doing it wrong. Captain Kennedy wrote a song about it entitled "Do Something Even If It's Wrong."

*Learning is a constant flow of problem solving experiences driven by the reality that failure is not only an option but an integral tool, guiding students on their pathway to success. Why shouldn't school be the same?*

To clear away the land mines from the pathway to success for every child, we first recognize that children are not the same and that learning is complex and individual. Be mindful that as the philosophy is being developed, it is critical for the reader to understand specifically how students will learn and progress through this system. The ideas presented are not a lesson to be followed but a philosophy that the readers may digest and make their own.

This is not a job for teachers who simply follow the text or the Common Core standards of teaching to the test. Educating our youth is a complex issue requiring the best teachers to pull out all their resources to teach every child as a unique individual. Highly qualified teachers who fully understand human growth and development, who have a concept of the need for individualization and are willing to put in hours of planning for every lesson are those who lead the way to reforming the reform movement. They are the ones who will take back their profession from those who simply teach to the test and toe the line with the textbook companies in an attempt to make all children identical.

## Age Levels, Not Grade Levels, Domino #3

Under this plan, grade levels become age levels no longer based on academic achievement. It is no longer necessary to fail students back to a whole new age level as promotion is based on passing authentic assessments, not moving from grade to grade. This is the third domino to fall. The goal is to allow students to be comfortable within their age groups for optimal success. From these age-level groupings, teams are developed. It is obvious that the teams will not be homogeneous by design. Assessments become presentations and can happen as a group or for individuals on various levels. Either way they check off a proficiency when they are successful and move on to the next. It will be necessary to provide individualization within the teams, allowing differentiated instruction to take place in many forms.

## Differentiated Instruction, Domino #4

Differentiated instruction as defined by Carol Ann Tomlinson means "tailoring instruction to meet individual needs. Whether teachers differentiate content, process, products, or the learning environment, the use of ongoing assessment and flexible grouping makes this a successful approach to instruction"

The goal is to empower teachers to take students from "where they are" to success, and to empower them to reach their highest goals, no matter what it takes. This strategy is designed to give teachers the flexibility to focus on student needs and respond to them. With this structure, the freedom to teach is coupled with the freedom to learn, assuring success to every individual student. This, the fourth domino, becomes essential to the success of the proficiency checklist.

Differentiated instruction comes in many packages. Most recently computerized programs have been designed to meet the specific needs of children functioning on many levels. This is great but, under this philosophy of education, students are to be active working on projects, getting into the community, presenting exhibitions, and so forth. Computer based instruction is one piece of the puzzle or one station as students rotate into many educational experiences.

A second station could easily be "centers." This would be a small group of students who are performing on the same level working on an assignment relative to all. Mix this in with a third station where students are working on a project. A good example would be a science fair or a fund-raising project for a needy organization.

Projects allow students to have specific assignments aligned with their goals as defined on their MAP. Projects have great flexibility and can incorporate many different subjects. Perhaps a fourth station would take a small group of students into the community to enhance learning. This is a great role for the education assistant remembering again all activities are based on the students MAP goals.

This is a sampling of how the process of differentiated instruction would allow all students to reach their specific goals. There are many more

innovative ideas that can be utilized. The good news is that teachers can innovate to their hearts desire, no longer tied to a script or common goals but set
free to focus on every child as an individual. The teachers, in the trenches,
are the only ones who completely understand the needs of their students. This
cannot be done from afar.

This is a difficult task. Probably the most difficult challenge a professional
educator will ever face. But that is why teachers are professionals. Those who
simply follow the text might want to step back and let the leaders lead. Once
in place, it will be very difficult for teachers, parents, or students to go back
to the ways of the past. They will become addicted to innovation. Not to mention, once the dominos start to fall, there is no stopping them.

Politicians will have to step out of the way because the train has left the station. Either get on board or get run over. There are no rules against what has been
suggested here, just past practices frozen in place by agenda driven politicians.

## The Map to Graduation, Domino #5

Under the current system students are expected to graduate somewhere near
their eighteenth birthday. Those who have previously failed, see the hopelessness as their future age of graduation drifts into the twenty-plus category.
They certainly don't want to feel out of place as a twenty-year-old in school,
and it is questionable whether schools would accept them. If it is unlikely
they will graduate anyway, why stay in school?

To stop this process from destroying children, we must look at how we
can move students forward at their own rate and in their own direction. Now
it becomes more important "that" they will graduate rather than "when" they
will graduate. This is the fifth domino. The process along the way, from kin-
dergarten on up, must be designed to enforce students' individual pathway to
success allowing them to move forward to completion. This will require team
work by all teachers be they at the primary, middle, or secondary school level.

It is evident that as students move through a system at different rates, some
will go to college or other post-graduation destinations at a younger age
and some will graduate from high school at an older age. Today's process
for graduation is the number one reason for the huge student dropout rates.
Graduation is determined by Carnegie units, a relic designed in the late nine-
teenth to early twentieth centuries to assure students had enough seat time to
graduate. The Carnegie Institute is no longer connected with the units. Success in achieving these units is determined by students passing the tests and
the class, taught in a singular manner and learning at the same time.

If a fundamental educational philosophy incorporates a true acceptance
that students learn at different rates, it will be necessary to allow graduation at different times. This change will remove a time constraint that forces

some students to drop out by limiting their ability to graduate past a certain age. When planning, and updating the MAP for each student the multiple pathways for graduation must be discussed. It is essential that the student has information that enhances their best chances of success in their future lives.

To accomplish this, it is necessary to expand our horizons, to again erase from our mind the way schools are supposed to be and look to the future, the way schools should be. Begin by attaching high school classes to a wide range of community colleges, technical schools, charter schools, and specialty schools for those students passing the age of twenty and still working toward their graduation.

Alternative programs could then be made available to an ever-increasing number of students. These options would be designed for ongoing students or those who have temporarily dropped out and are returning based on a specialty they might want to study. If the public education system is to exist, adjustments must be made to meet the needs of all children and adults wishing to become educated for their future.

When Matt returned from the Navy back in 1958, he went back to high school to graduate. He looked a little out of place but he didn't seem to mind at all. He was able to do well in the subject areas but, more importantly, he passed on knowledge from his experiences to his new classmates. It was amazing when he built a one-seat helicopter for his shop project … that worked!

Alvin went back to school in a poverty-stricken country at age twenty. In order to attend a reasonable school, he had to pay a fee. He had no access to money and wasn't able to attend. After being out for two years he returned to play sports and finish his secondary education.

Both are success stories. Matt got his diploma and proceeded to work a good job and live a comfortable life. Alvin went to college on a basketball scholarship and graduated. In both cases, they graduated when they were ready. No longer were they dropouts. There are many more stories waiting to be told. Significant to the school design, graduation must indicate that students have learned no matter how long it has taken them to complete the proficiencies.

Now the question arises, in what age range will students be able to remain in a specific traditional school building or class? It may not be a good idea to have adults sitting in class with third graders. First, they wouldn't want to be embarrassed and second, the teaching techniques would be entirely different. That is why grade levels are not used as indicators of promotion, but indicators of age levels. Keep students with their peers where they have similar social skills and experiences.

Under the new plan, students will remain in the school program while promotion is determined by their success. This would not necessarily mean the students would be in the same building however. The local school districts will determine, along with the student, who will remain in the original school and who will move on to a new location. This all depends on the comfort level of the school and student. They make that decision together. No matter where the student goes, the MAP will follow.

This alternative site would then become an extension of their original public school. Transitioning to this type of progressive learning would not be difficult as alternative schools already exist throughout the country. Actually, this would be ideal for charter schools collaborating with traditional public schools in the best interest of the child. This exemplifies the need for community colleges which could serve students at the high school, college or vocational training level forming a smooth transition for those who were previously hopeless.

Another example is a program that is in place and running now. The Job Corps has been available for a long time. Here students finish high school and are able to learn a specific skill in the process. A good example is the Horizon Youth Services in the Muhlenberg Career Development Center in Greenville, Kentucky. This school is specially designed to prepare students to operate heavy machinery. At this time, students may attend up to age twenty-four.

Students may be working on their high school diploma along with the desired skill or they may enter with a completed MAP and seek out the skills of their interest. Under this new plan, those seeking a diploma would carry with them their MAP and the education center receiving them will assure it is followed. As Job Corps locations are already in place throughout the United States, this alliance could easily be an integral part of the education norm. Expansion of Job Corps could easily follow the current model, based on job needs on a national level.

As long as students are in school at any of these locations, they are not dropouts and they still have a future. Not only does the MAP go with the students, it is followed through graduation and into employment. There should be no age limits on learning.

Imagine a university being able to see a prospective students MAP of actual accomplishments rather than an artificial diploma, an SAT score or grade point averages. And a prospective employer would have similar abilities. So often a diploma is used to end a child's education, to push them out of school lacking skills needed for their future. This makes a diploma irrelevant. The MAP will now be the indicator of completion.

*Universities as well as potential employers have specific skill requirements for acceptance. Now they can determine whether a student, leaving the system of education, is prepared.*

## Focusing on the Advanced Student, Domino #6

Those who move faster through the system must not be forgotten. The sixth domino allows those with accelerated learning to be empowered to move forward, at their best rate even if it means entering college at a younger age. Will they continue to be held back re-learning information they already know? Will they receive a fake "A" that builds their ego but proves that they haven't been challenged? Our plan doesn't have letter grades so egos must be stroked by the actual development of skills. Shouldn't our highest skilled students be challenged so they can learn from failure, WD-40 style?

The same policy applies to those who move faster as it does to those who move slower. Since they have their MAP, and that MAP is reviewed on a regular basis by the student, parents, and educators, it is unlikely that the student will be left in the shadows, forced to perform in a substandard way. Those who have exemplary skills in a particular subject area must be allowed to fully blossom.

Many schools have advanced university level classes within their buildings. That is a good thing as long as the student will be challenged. But that may not be enough. When there is a nearby university, community college, or on-line classes, this advanced student will have the opportunity to shine. And that can be done for one class or more, depending on the needs of the student.

## Evolving of Special Education, Domino #7

During a conversation regarding this new philosophy, the question will arise, where do students with special needs fit in? This group, often forgotten or pushed to the side, will fit perfectly into the new system of education thus lending itself as the seventh domino. Remember, we now take children from "where they are," following their MAP and serving the needs of all. And what is a MAP? It is a simpler version of an IEP, an Individual Education Plan, used to guide the students with special needs on their pathway to success. Now everyone has that MAP/IEP and students with special needs are no longer branded on their foreheads for all to see.

Special education has evolved over the years but has never seemed to settle in as an integral part of the total education system. It has always been perceived as an asterisk to the general education provided. In the 1970s-special education was becoming an issue of interest for the first time. New laws were being written to assure students with special needs had a free and appropriate education. Although people were supportive of this effort, few understood its implications.

During that time a school in Milwaukee Wisconsin called Pleasant View, serviced over 200 students with a variety of special needs. Every student had an individual plan and a new school was built with modern facilities. But of significance was that, although many praised the school few understood it. And fewer paid attention to what was going on in the school. That was great because it allowed for innovation without interference.

At Pleasant View School, miracles were accomplished. All 200 plus students had individual plans and a systemic philosophy to assure success. Every child was different and that was understood. But could that exist for all students in a normalized setting? Concepts from that school were used and broadened in the 1990s to develop the Milwaukee Village School, a school designed for all children and serving a general education population. This school design showed how students with special needs fit in to the overall flow of education.

These schools were designed within the traditional system regardless of how bad that system was. Implementation was on a clandestine level with trickery and deceit utilized on a regular basis. As the saying goes, it is easier to ask forgiveness than to get permission. The experiences at these two schools show that these concepts are not just a dream. They are realities waiting to happen.

Special education took a turn for the worse with the advent of the No Child Left Behind law as well as Common Core. A primary source of the cata-strophic problem is the legal conflict between the Individual Education Plan (IEP) and the rigid timelines of Common Core culminating with a meaningless standardized test. With two separate sets of goals blended into one for convenience, the strong emphasis placed on the "test" has diminished the value of the IEP. The teacher is handcuffed by the demands placed on students to be successful on the "test" and thus distracted away from their true needs. This isn't only unethical, it is illegal!

## Blending in the IEP

Under this new system, special education will exist as a critical part of the total education process in the school; however, it will be nearly invisible to the casual observer. All students enter the school with the goal of improvement, including those with documented special needs. The special-education teacher will guide the MAP / IEP of their students and oversee their program but will work with all students based on their needs.

As all students are assured of an appropriate education through the MAP, students with special needs are not the anomaly; they are simply an extension of the norm. Students enter the school building as "students." This means no educators would be referred to publicly as special-education teachers, no rooms identified as special-education rooms, and no students would be publicly referred to by their area of exceptionality. Some students will display behaviors that are outside the norm, of course, but as far as the professional staff is concerned, the fact that a student has special-education needs will be completely confidential.

## Inclusion Made Real

The fiasco of inclusion will be the first to be rearranged under this new plan. It isn't enough to force students away from their individual goals into that standardized box, but to have them enter a classroom and receive a form of general education which is not even effective for general education students is unacceptable.

When all students have a plan in the form of the MAP, all student needs are foremost in the minds of educators, whatever they may be. In the new plan, inclusion will be turned upside down as all students will be received in a routine manner. They will proceed to teams with the expectation that students and educators alike will not only treat them in an appropriate manner but will be sensitive to their needs.

If any students have a specific area of need within this less restrictive classroom, they could, for example, be pulled out into small groups to meet that need. Pull-outs would be based solely on student needs and that includes students who have no special-education needs by definition. Pull-outs would not then be noticed as simply for those diagnosed, but all students would blend in and confidentiality would be maintained. Pull-outs would also be used to provide small groups utilizing differentiated learning. Those with special needs would fit in perfectly.

Of course, there are students whose needs include a more restrictive setting. This would be honored as would all recommendations in the IEP / MAP. The least restrictive environment is mandated by the IEP / MAP and will be adhered to not just for students with special needs, but for all students. If any student needs the support of a more restricted environment, whether for a short or long term, that is what they will receive.

## Scrap the Crap, Domino #8

We now address the most important issue before us known as the eighth domino. As the process of whole child reform is put into place, it becomes evident that the standardized test is meaningless if replaced by the proficiency checklist, authentic assessments, and the small pre-and post-test.

Now remember, if the testing police are checking on you, your activities must be clandestine. Parents of kindred minds can be very helpful because they can't be fired. They have the ability to mingle with other parents and family members to pass the word that the test is the least valuable of all assessments. A good assessment doesn't just give a score, it gives detailed information about a child's progress, what a child can actually accomplish, not just with paper and pencil in hand but with demonstrations of learning. But most of all, parents will pass the word that there is a better idea.

There may be parents who are convinced that the test is important. That's alright, we must respect their wishes. When it comes time for their children to take the test, tell them to not worry about it, have fun, and come back to the joy of learning when they are done. As our teaching methods will improve the skills of the students anyway, they should do well. Remember not to put children in the middle of the conflict. Having fun with a test and not worrying about it is a good strategy to relax children, they will probably do better anyway. Teachers, however, must simply ignore the existence of the test for all practical purposes. Don't do artificial test prep or any other "teach to the test" nonsense.

The sabotage is complete when the test comes back. By the time the results are in, the child has months of progress. Remind the parents that by then the test is out of date. Extremely important is to use this time to show the parents your ongoing assessments and how timely they are. A teacher's classroom information is much more valuable to help understand what skills need to be taught to the students. Show them the facts, not letter grades, not a count of homework completed, not a test score, but an explanation of the skills their children demonstrated.

## Assessment by Exhibition

The days of the chapter test are over. A demonstration of learning is often the best way to assess what students really know. The exhibition is one way of assessing students by demonstrating their skills in the way they do it best. It may take the form of a speech, a play, a song, a debate, a project or any other means by which the student can truly show what they can do, in the way they do it best. We begin by assuring teachers have a full understanding of the concept of the exhibition. Here's a plan for teachers:

Objective: Teachers will be responsible for teaching the students about exhibitions.

- Teachers will understand that exhibitions are an activity used for students to demonstrate learned proficiencies.
- Teachers will understand that exhibitions will be used to provide a culminating activity for closure and a partial final assessment of a thematic unit.
- Teachers will provide examples of a creative exhibition to students.
- Teachers will brainstorm with students about other possible activities to present.
- Teachers will encourage students to take ownership of the activity.

Teachers and staff will act as facilitators and then step aside to let the students shine. It may take a few exhibitions for the students to get the real idea, but soon they will know how to take the reins and will amaze the audience with what they have learned.

Objective: To provide an avenue for students to show and tell about their learning experiences.

- Teams of students will prepare a presentation geared to a concept specifically designed to meet their MAP objectives.
- Exhibitions will be presented on a regular basis, usually as a culminating activity of a unit.
- Teams of students choose their preferred method to demonstrate learning.
- Students are to meet and prepare the entire presentation.
- The students work together to create a set: an agora or marketplace, or whatever environment they would need within the school or without.
- A wide range of skills are utilized in every exhibition. Involvement would include everyone based on their assessment needs as determined in their MAP.
- The students prepare a script for the production.
- A student moderator is chosen by the group.
- The students practice the exhibition, with one student acting as the producer.
- Parents and community representatives may be invited.
- Students will improve their presentation skills throughout the year.
- Students will have pride and remember what they have learned.
- Assessment will be based on the observation of skills demonstrated.
- Students make a video recording of the production, so they can critique themselves and improve their skills.
- Students document the event by completing a "What I Learned" form which is placed in their portfolio.

A self-assessment is essential in empowering students to progress on their proficiency checklist to reinforce their view of what they learned. When they return home after school and are asked what they learned, they will actually be able to answer in a reasonable manner. Here are some sample questions and answers:

State the specific role that I played in this exhibition: "I helped make the set, the costumes and was the moderator for this Exhibition."
What proficiency did I exhibit? "Analytical Thinking"
Math: "I designed and measuring the cloth for my costume."

Communication Skills:

*Speaking:* "I prepared and delivered a commentary within the setting of a play."
*Reading:* "I researched the history related to my role in the play."
*Writing:* "I wrote out my script"
*Listening:* "I listened to other cast members to better understand how my character fit into the overall play."

Rank yourself on how well you did on this activity. Rubrics are developed based on the need of the activity:

• Eye contact was appropriate.
• Speaking was loud and articulate.
• Posture displayed confidence.
• Command of the language was demonstrated.

Many other issues could easily be a part of the self-assessment. Most important is for the student to look inward and recognize what they did well and where they "failed." As with WD-40, that failure then becomes part of the learning process.

## Assessing Critical Thinking

The question arises how do we assess critical thinking? With critical thinking the importance is not who wins or loses, it is what is learned and what will be learned from the failures that are now positive learning experiences. Assessing a project includes a wide range of methods to demonstrate skills and abilities. Of significance is to assess this project, not with letter grades but with observations of every aspect of the child's performance with a special emphasis on their MAP objectives.

In assessing critical thinking, we now take note of what Dr. Angela Dye referred to as A level learning to develop an assessment outline.

• Analyzing
  ◦ Define the central issues of the problem.
  ◦ Fully understand the complexity of the problem.
  ◦ Determine resources needed to resolve the issue at hand.
  ◦ Research the problem.
• Synthesizing
  ◦ Ask pertinent questions relative to the problem.
  ◦ Identify arguments on all sides of the issue.
  ◦ Make self-corrections.

- ○ Correctly interpret data.
- • Applying
  - ○ Identifying flaws in arguments.
  - ○ Make the case for your designated argument.
  - ○ Draw and support valid conclusions.
  - ○ Examples and facts are given to support reasons, with references.
  - ○ Work as a team to demonstrate or present conclusions.
- • Evaluating
  - ○ Evaluating the reliability of evidence.
  - ○ Evaluate the validity of your conclusions.
  - ○ Work with a team of evaluators to come to a consensus.

What if the teacher told the class they will be doing a project and that an indicator of success might very well be the number of failures that lead to the final solution? Of course, the students would want to do the easiest project. But what if the teacher indicated that more failures would lead to a better rating for the project? Would the students now be more inclined to take on a more complex project? Every student must be challenged to reach their ultimate level of achievement.

When the agenda driven politicians try to draw you back to a testing mentality, remind them that we can assess orchestra competitions, forensics meets, singers on "The Voice," science fairs, speeches, and many more activities in a meaningful way. The test is the worst way to determine a student's skills.

## The Freedom to Teach, Domino #9

Of significant importance is that teachers are empowered to take charge of their classroom and beyond. In this plan, teachers work in teams. As such, they are given the flexibility to create groupings that best fit the learning styles of their students. Students may be grouped by abilities at times, while at other times grouped by interest. They may also be grouped according to a specific skill they need to develop. As students go into the community for real life experiences, this flexibility allows for small groups while others may work in projects that are receptive to larger groups. Teachers make those decisions.

More to the point, teachers are fully empowered to teach. If they needed a class period to last ninety minutes, it will happen within their team block of time as the teachers make that decision. If a shorter period of time is preferable, teachers would also make that decision. If they want to take their students into the community for the whole day, that could be arranged by the team without any alterations to the school schedule. No substitute teachers, no teachers covering classes, just clear it with administration, pick up and go. Given that the community is considered a part of the classroom, and that is signed off on at the beginning of the year by parents, no new permission slips are needed as long as the activities are routine, and parents are informed.

At Village School teacher Catherine Spivey and her team decided to spend the whole week on a science project. This project took students into the community to test the waters of Lake Michigan, get on the computer to team with schools around the lake, in Michigan, Illinois, Indiana and Wisconsin, and to research thus integrating a wide variety of academics. She didn't need any special arrangements, they just got the "go ahead" from this administrator, and off they went.

This was at the middle school level but, with adaptations and a whole bunch of creativity, High School and Elementary Schools could be this flexible.

*The empowerment of teachers to teach is the most invigorating aspect of the profession. Never again will teachers be able to go back to the old way of teaching.*

## ESSENTIALS FOR FULL IMPLEMENTATION

Implementation of this plan will not be easy. We must dig deep into our creative juices with teachers supporting teachers to provide an atmosphere for creativity. With your team of invested stakeholders on board the change we wish for will become a reality.

### Class Size Matters

The current policies of the Department of Education appear to embrace artificial competition through the increase of charter schools as a driving force in the effort to promote the rhetoric of reform. To counter this sabotage of the public-school system, educators must insist on an even playing field. When money is shifted away from traditional public schools, a reasonable class size becomes more difficult to maintain.

Clearly the current policies are on a track to fail unless substantial changes are made to allow for real innovation. Fundamental to a quality school system is the ability of the teachers to focus on the individual needs of a widely diverse population of students. Implementing differentiated learning, essential to innovation, is hampered, if not destroyed by huge class sizes making it easy for the politically driven educators to force failure onto schools.

How can an individualized system be accomplished with class sizes of 45 to 50 or more? Right now, the alternative for many teachers is to throw out education for children to catch in a bushel basket or follow a standardized script. Others do their best to innovate under unspeakable conditions. The demands of previous reforms required individualization. They require that no child be left behind but they put a teacher into a classroom where they are forced to leave children behind. That's where the politicians must look at reality rather than their agenda. It's time to embrace the agenda of children, and that means providing a class environment that allows teachers to do their job.

To accomplish this the teacher must become an advocate, speaking out not only about class size as a general statement but armed with a box full of ideas that can be implemented once the class size is brought down to a realistic level. Instead of standing silent, following a script as presented by Common Core, take a stand in the classroom and beyond. It is unethical and even immoral to be silent when the best interest of students is the issue. Teachers along with parents are the closest to the child, and if they can't advocate, who can?

This effort will take courage. As much as politicians will try to frame it to look like teachers are trying to make their job easier, the reality is evident that children can be taught better when given individual attention. Class size around seventeen can enhance learning dramatically.

There are creative ways to improve class size at little extra cost. Along with that box full of ideas, creative strategies to reduce class size must be in your cache of wisdom. A wise use of educational assistants is one. Imagine a team of two teachers, an educational assistant and a special-education teacher with a double class load of sixty. That would be thirty per class. That group of students can be broken up into four groups of fifteen for best results. It can also be divided in many ways based on the need of that day's lesson.

Well placed educational assistants are a great asset to the learning process. Requirements must be that they have taken education courses and ideally are continuing their education to become a teacher. That way a school can develop home-grown teachers familiar with their school and philosophy. With the addition of educational assistants as well as sufficient teachers, the class load must be reduced to a level that is workable.

## Planning for Success

Keep in mind that the current policies presented by the US Department of Education as well as the State are destined to fail. With no noticeable pathway to innovation, educators must begin the process of changing the system from the bottom up. To advocate for meeting the individual needs of children, teachers must be allowed to prepare for those needs daily. Providing for a quality education takes planning and planning takes time.

Extending sitting time in a class does nothing to improve the quality of learning, nor does it help a student progress. Sitting time, directed toward memorization, is simply sitting time. What is significant is the time that can be spent focusing on specific needs of individual students. Differentiated learning requires every child to have a well thought out plan of action. Projects that have students working on their specific proficiencies are a good example. Every minute in the education setting must be well utilized. There is no such thing as wasted time.

Education seems easy for those who believe the teacher's job is to stay one chapter ahead of the students in the textbook or to follow a script. But that simplistic approach has failed children for centuries. Every child is different with a different brain and a different set of background information. Accordingly, every child needs a plan, and planning takes time.

If there is any doubt about the necessity of planning, ask a television anchor who spends one hour on the air. What do they do with the rest of the day? Anything worthwhile takes an effort, and that is different for different people. But differentiated learning, essential to a quality education, takes a great deal of planning and re-planning and some of that planning must be done as a team with colleagues. As previously described, putting three teachers and an educational assistant together in the best interest of children requires communication.

The professional educator must be armed with a cadre of great ideas to present to their leaders. It will not be popular but one approach that would not cost any money is to reduce the student day. Educators know that quality learning time is more important than sitting time, but this will be a difficult sell.

There is another suggestion that might soften the blow. That is the use of Community Learning Center's to enhance education for every student. Many are in place throughout the country but here are some thoughts as to how they can support learning. A daily, after school learning center can coordinate with teachers to assure a student's educational plan is reinforced. In addition, the center would be active during every school vacation. This would be available to those parents and students who choose to use it. The student's educational plan will be reinforced, and valuable student time will be increased.

*In the early 1970's many marched on the picket line, placing their jobs in danger, to assure quality pay for teachers. This may be the time for all teachers, nationwide, to go on the picket line to assure a small class size and planning time in the best interest of the students.*

*Chapter 8*

# Replacing Fake Accountability

Teacher assessment is only as good as the information gathered and its application to the betterment of the quality of education. Its purpose is not to get rid of teachers based on an administrator's lust for power, nor is it to force them into compliance with an outdated system of education. It is to improve the quality of education while continuing to allow those professionals to have a voice in the educational process without fear of reprisal.

A new view of teacher accountability is essential to improving the quality of the system of education. The reality is that current accountability measures are based on the unethical "teach to the test" mentality that ultimately silences innovators while forcing them to follow scripted lessons. As most administrators have no time to do a full professional assessment, they seek the easiest path to achieve their goals. They look at test scores or other "snapshot" views of the teacher.

Given that assessment is essential for professional growth and that quality assessment rarely happens under the current system of education, it is time to subvert the process. For those lucky enough to have a union, it might be a good time to collaborate with them along with a local university to re-design assessment to be a more highly valued tool.

## TEACHER ASSESSMENT FOR ACCOUNTABILITY

The question of accountability is extremely important to parents and educators. No one wants a teacher in their school who is doing damage to children. To begin the process of whole child reform, the state standardized test must be abandoned as an assessment tool. It is not an indicator of the value of a teacher or a school. There are way too many variables affecting student out come such as environmental causes, student physical and mental health, as well as natural differences in all human beings. The list goes on and on. Without the test, however, how do we assure our children have quality teachers? This is a complex issue and there is no way to simplify it.

## Taking Politics Out of the Mix

We must begin by taking politics out of teacher assessment. It is important to recognize that school administrators have their hands full managing a school and lack sufficient time to properly assess a teacher. In addition, the perception of politics, in the past has created an atmosphere of mistrust leading to the belief that teacher assessment is punitive.

When focus is on the children, we recognize the value of having the best teachers in the classroom. We also recognize that the development of a quality teacher is a process that requires support while they are on the job. They can only learn so much at the university. Like all professions, growth happens on an incremental basis, while doing the job. And the best teachers never stop growing.

To resolve this issue, consideration may be given to using retired teachers and administrators to assume these duties. The costs would be significantly less than hiring more administrators and they would be able to spend more time in the classroom. In addition, they would be more suited to understanding the needs of the teacher and available to help when needed. Those who believe that retired teachers would be soft on their counterparts are simply wrong. History has shown that they would have no hesitation to recommend that administrators "pull the plug" if a teacher was unsuccessful. Rarely is it that a retired educator would tolerate an unsatisfactory teacher in the classroom.

To assure quality, connect this group of assessors with a university, a related non-profit, or other competent organization that will oversee them and will assure accurate results. This separate entity would allow sufficient time to make quality assessments as well as an unbiased approach to the teachers involved. These issues must become top priority for this plan to work.

Personnel must be available to assess a teacher's skills, as well as support the teacher in improving the ability to connect educational lessons with students. Quality teachers will be able to teach in the way they teach best and those file cabinets filled with creative ideas, now gathering dust, will once again be used. Each thoughtful, well-planned lesson, structured for the students' needs, will be more successful in conveying its content. There is a tremendous amount of talent available in this profession, let it be fully utilized.

Essential to developing this innovative program is to ensure teachers are taking the right approach in the classroom to promote change. To assure quality teaching, it is important to guarantee teachers follow the best innovative ideas in their areas of expertise. To provide a quality lesson, in this new philosophy, teachers must be ready for a magnitude of planning related to daily activities. It should never be forgotten that the teacher is the professional. They drive the lesson daily. However, some mandates must be in place.

## Assessing Teachers

Essential to this philosophy, the teacher must come to every class prepared. A long-range plan connecting lesson plans to units, and units to demonstrated proficiencies must lead in a specific direction to ensure student achievement. No longer will teachers follow the text verbatim. They will finally be allowed to become the professionals they were educated to be. Goals and objectives driving teacher assessment must be made clear:

- Planning:
  - Teachers will come to the classroom thoroughly prepared, with a strong focus on individual student growth.
  - Thematic units will be in place and connected to general standards.
  - Unit plans will clearly and methodically map out strategies for a theme.
  - Lesson Plans will be thorough focusing on student differences and will be utilized daily. These plans will be available to assessors to assure quality planning.
  - Student Learning Plans (MAP) will be in place, driving each student's education.
  - All community experiences and other activities will be well-planned and incorporated into lesson plans.

Teaching strategies will be developed to fit into this new philosophy. Many of these strategies are already being used by quality teachers on a regular basis but the new system creates a vital environment where innovation is actively encouraged.

- Teaching strategies:
  - Differentiated instruction is a top priority.
  - Teachers will teach in the way students learn best.
  - Activities are developed with the student in the lead.
  - Well-designed projects meet the needs of students at different levels.
  - Well-designed community experiences meet the needs of all students.
  - Community experiences are preceded by student research, student planning, and preparatory lessons.

- ○ Community experiences are followed by student self-assessment, student presentations, student reflections, and wrap-up.
- ○ Lessons utilize questioning to promote critical thinking.
- ○ Integrated curriculum includes two or more core subjects with lesson plans and goals for each.
- ○ Community partners are utilized in developing community experiences, bringing the community into the classroom and providing expertise on specific issues.
- ○ Students are provided the opportunity to generalize as part of the daily learning activities.
- ○ A culminating activity is utilized to ensure all lessons connect with reality.
- ○ Teachers use multi-sensory approach to learning including visual, auditory, and kinesthetic instruction.
- ○ A variety of active lessons are incorporated into the planning. Some examples are role-playing, musical activities, art, dance, home economics, and shop.
- ○ Lessons connect with student background.
- ○ Lessons allow students to discover learning.
- ○ Teachers use assessment to drive the lesson.

The ability to communicate with students as well as colleagues is essential to a successful class. As technology expands, the ability to communicate through different types of media becomes more diverse, yet personal communication remains at the forefront.

- • Communication tools:
  - ○ Teachers will demonstrate the capability to communicate with students and staff in necessary ways.
  - ○ Technology is utilized to connect with the community and beyond to make student learning real.
  - ○ Assistive technology is used to promote student communication.
  - ○ Teachers will utilize non-verbal communication.
  - ○ Teachers will communicate in a most effective manner.

One of the most important areas in education is to recognize the diverse backgrounds, environments, cultures, and learning styles that each student possesses. There will be many areas of education where groups of students will have a commonality.

- • Diversity
  - ○ Accommodations are made for all students.

- A students' individual culture is considered in the planning of a lesson.
- Students' needs are met through appropriate pull-outs from the team for homogeneous groupings, especially in reading and math.
- Differentiated instruction is utilized to meet students' diverse needs.
- Teachers will acknowledge ideas from different perspectives, including a variety of cultures and belief systems.
- Lessons incorporate students' prior experiences.
- Lessons meet the interest needs of students.
- Lessons are planned to connect with the MAP of every student.

Rather than a one size fits all philosophy of education, this new system recognizes that children grow and develop differently. The teacher must recognize the stages of development and adjust teaching accordingly.

- Human growth and development:
  - Teachers will demonstrate understanding of how students learn in different ways and different rates.
  - Teachers will incorporate student MAPs as working documents.
  - Teachers use their knowledge of multiple intelligences to appropriately utilize student skills.
  - Teachers will prepare developmentally appropriate lessons.
  - Teachers will utilize background knowledge of student.

Educators will take ownership of the innovative philosophy and will continue to implement new ideas. The intention is to continually move forward to meet the needs of an ever-changing society.

- Innovation:
  - Teachers will examine their methods of teaching daily and create new ways to successfully allow learning to happen.
  - Students are put in the lead on a regular basis.
  - Teachers will implement the new system and philosophy of education until it is simply a part of the routine.
  - Teachers will have the courage to abandon past practices which have not proved successful while moving forward using new practices.

This new system and philosophy of education takes a "no holds barred" approach to maintaining the health and safety of the students. It goes way beyond the student discipline of the past. Although many of the successful strategies of the past will continue, there will be added efforts that are implemented in the classroom before students get to the level where stronger discipline is needed.

- Proactive planning
  - A well-planned, active curriculum is in place daily.
  - Planned activities fill the entire allotted time to allow for no down time.
  - All students are acknowledged for their success.
  - The daily routine has students welcomed into class in a consistent manner.
  - Lessons flow smoothly as non-verbal communication and other techniques redirect students when needed.
  - Teachers are proactive in potential crises situations.
  - Administration will provide non-violent crises intervention such as presented in organizations like the Crises Prevention Institute.
- Student behavior
  - Class rules are established with students in the lead.
  - Teachers provide an active class that leaves little or no "down time."
  - Teachers approach students in a positive manner.
  - Teachers are observant for signs of potential conflict.
  - Teachers recognize that the first step in de-escalating a crisis is being supportive.
  - Teachers resolve issues on the class level whenever possible.
  - Teachers respect the privacy of students as they avoid reprimanding in public.
  - A behavior plan/contract is created when necessary, by the teaching team, parents, and students. This connects with the students MAP as necessary. It is eliminated totally when successful.

Assessment is an integral part of the new philosophy. This will drive the lessons of the students daily. This process must be ongoing and documented in an effective manner to assure student success.

- Assessment:
  - Teachers will use the most effective assessment tools to gain information to drive the curriculum for the students.
  - Teachers use technology for efficient record-keeping.
  - Teachers maintain portfolios to monitor student progress.
  - Teachers record ongoing anecdotal notes based on daily student observations.
  - Teachers document demonstrations of learning on the proficiency check list.
  - Teachers involve students in self-assessment.
  - Teachers report progress in a meaningful way.
  - Teachers implement additional creative assessments.

A certain policy that is seemingly forgotten in industry as well as education is remembering the customer. The customers are the parents, and they must be treated accordingly. This is not only when dealing with an issue of concern but is also by recognizing that they know more about their child than any of the educators. Their information is crucial to the success of their children.

- Parental Involvement:
  - Teachers will involve parents in a meaningful way, not only as the customer, but as the students' first teacher.
  - Teachers maintain regular contact with all parents.
  - Teachers report accurately to parents with positive, negative, and neutral information.
  - Teachers survey parents on a regular basis to gather information.
  - Teachers support parents with student activities to be implemented at home.

The importance of bringing education up to date is only overshadowed by the importance of keeping education up to date. As new ideas come forth, educators must keep abreast of the information provided and move the profession forward on a regular basis.

- Teacher self-improvement:
  - Teachers will set annual goals to research and read about current issues in the educational field, participate in professional activities, support school projects, and collaborate with colleagues.
  - Teachers demonstrate the ability to work with a team.
  - Teacher ensures all students' MAPs are followed.
  - Teachers develop a philosophy of teaching.
  - Teachers are aware of the legal aspects of education; that is, Mandated Reporter, Tort Collaboration.
  - Teachers collaborate with colleagues on student issues.
  - Teachers are involved in school-related activities.
  - Teachers attend workshops or classes for self-improvement.
  - Teachers present at workshops, classes, etc.
  - Teachers do self-evaluation of annual goals.

The indicator of teacher success would be their ability to adapt to the needs of students, allowing them to get on track and move forward.

# HOW DO TESTS FIT INTO THE PICTURE?

With the huge standardized test out of the picture, we look to find a replacement that will have an even playing field and will give a snap shot of student progress in a timely manner, to teachers. Begin by replacing the big test with small pre-and post-tests. Those tests should take no longer than twenty or thirty minutes and given one on one to assure accuracy. Couple student results on those tests with authentic teacher assessments and you're on your way to a more informative assessment. If that shows many students in a class or a team advancing slower than their past records indicate, there might be reason to be concerned. This is not valid, of course, unless the ultimate purpose is to provide quality information to the teacher.

A student's past record of individual tests, confirmed by teacher's authentic assessments, will allow progress to be charted to determine if the student had previously reached the levels that the school is now seeing. For example, if a school has a strong majority of children gaining one grade level in reading and that progress had never been seen before, don't let anyone tell you that school or the teachers are failures. Conversely, if many children have made consistent gains in the past and are now floundering, there is reason for concern.

This is a complex issue that will require critical thinking to determine the cause of the problem of low student achievement. It is never the teacher alone. Teachers teaming with counselors or social workers, for example, might need to visit homes of students to determine if anything has dramatically changed either there or in their neighborhood. Have there been any recent changes within the school environment?

There are many more concerns to explore. After all issues are considered, a full teacher assessment may be necessary to determine if the teacher or team of teachers are using the quality strategies needed to support student success. To achieve this, it is essential that all assessments are based on an even playing field.

The information from the small test is only a portion of the complete assessment. It is compared to the entire assessment and recommendations are given for improvement. After several complete assessments over a period of time, the teacher will have opportunity to show growth and that will be extremely satisfying. On the occasion that a teacher does not rise to a standard, due process will be evident.

*Most teachers are appreciative of the information gathered and growth is evident. Those who did not grow, often realized they were in the wrong profession.*

# BRINGING INTEGRITY BACK TO
# SCHOOL ACCOUNTABILITY

Replacing the old-time school accountability plan with one that assures all children will have a quality education is a most difficult feat. It is difficult because many politicians have preconceived notions about what a school should be.

We must subvert the failed school assessment system as well as the mentality that drives that system. While assessment should be complex, it is simplified for the convenience of those politicians who prefer short cuts, like artificial graduation rates that are easy to camouflage. It is much easier to point to a test score than to take the time to fully analyze achievement in a school.

When they present their artificial numbers, teachers must team with unions, parents, universities, and any organization that will support the truth. To hold schools accountable there must be a fair and honest assessment of that school. Every school has different students from different backgrounds with different abilities; however, there are essential fundamentals that can be documented and evaluated. Attention must be given to a little-known part of the "Every Student Succeeds Act" that allows for innovative assessments.

## Change is Afoot

Be aware that an effort is already in the works to secretly change and truly develop innovation in public education. Charters can join in if they choose because there are no children we want to see pushed away from education. Innovative education, following the agenda of children, is for everyone, working together supporting collaboration rather than competition.

To begin the change, we must open the door to creativity by looking at opportunities recently put in place. A significant amendment to the "Every Student Succeeds Act" is that made by Senator Susan Collins and Senator Bernie Sanders. The amendment passed with the final bill says in part:

1. "Innovative assessment" system defined:

The term "innovative assessment" system means a system of assessments that may include the following:

1. Competency-based assessments, instructionally embedded assessments, interim assessments, cumulative year end assessments, or performance-based assessments that combine into an annual summative

determination for a student which may be administered through computer adapted assessments AND

2. Assessments that validate when students are ready to demonstrate mastery or proficiency and allow for differentiated student support based on individual learning needs.

This portion of the bill has the potential of being a game changer. "Assessments that validate when students are ready to demonstrate mastery" clearly indicates that students can take the assessment, not simply when it was given, but on the student's time frame taking every child from "where they are." And if their educational plan leads to their proficiencies, then the curriculum will change drastically.

Included are performance-based assessments. Again, the curriculum must now prepare students to demonstrate learning, not simply take the test. The Empowerment Council members, being supportive of innovation, would guide your school to innovate in a way valuable to all students. Every member is an agent for change expanding a coalition incrementally.

## Adherence to an Innovative Philosophy

When an innovative philosophy is implemented in a school, there must be a team effort, with everyone on the same page to be fully involved. The failed system and philosophy of education leads to the necessity for innovation in every school. Assessing the quality of a school must allow that school to move forward to provide a system that serves all children. This new process will provide an outside assessor who will visit the school at regular intervals to assure the philosophy is being implemented on a regular basis.

A variety of surveys will be conducted to determine different perspectives on the quality and innovative success of the school philosophy. Parent and teacher survey questions will focus on the implementation process of the new concept that respects the intelligence and abilities of all children. General survey concerns to all groups will be determined by:

- Clarity of intent of the philosophy.
- Teachers are in tune with the new philosophy.
- The philosophy is consistent with the needs of the child.
- The philosophy meets the needs of students at all levels.

## No More Over-Testing

Essential to the new innovative philosophy is to replace the state test with small pre-and post-tests. As these tests are compared to ongoing classroom assessments, their accuracy is increased. If there is a contradiction, a meeting is held with a specialist or an administrator to resolve the issue. This is valuable to the teacher as a snap shot in time, to determine whether the student is over performing or under performing in class. Their purpose, combined with a wide range of assessment tools, is to assure students are progressing and a school is effective.

The test along with class assessments are used to monitor academic growth in the student, in one school, under the watchful eye of one teacher or team of teachers. Not only does that give a better assessment, it can be used to counter the generalizations made by the artificial state standardized test.

When the powers to be say that your students did not reach proficiency, you can counter with statements like "70% of the individual students gained one year plus and 80% of those had never done that before." This information demonstrates individual gains made regardless of the level of the students when they enter the school.

Under this plan there are no complicated formulas to give estimates of achievement. This is the real deal. Here we take actual individual results and compare them with previous individual results to assure students are progressing on a level playing field. This brings assessment to the local level where it has value to the student. Although given locally, the State must monitor the results to assure equity among all students.

A case for State and Federal involvement goes back to "Brown versus Board of Education" as there must be over-sight to allow fair treatment of all students, especially those who have been denied equal education in the past. As schools were desegregated, civil rights organizations such as the NAACP intensified their focus on fairness and equity in education. It is clear, going back to that era, the lack of fairness is an issue and must always be monitored.

To achieve equity, the State will continue to have an active role monitoring these test scores. However, the process is simply reversed. Instead of the State scoring the test and eventually sending the results to the school districts, the assessment is given locally with the results going immediately to the teachers and then to the State. In addition, these test scores have more validity simply because they are compared with the class assessments that are essential to the student's proficiency checklist. Assessment is built into the system and is ongoing, monitoring achievement throughout the years, the ultimate accountability.

The beauty of these small tests is that any educator can give them. To assure every child gets these tests one on one, simply use those educators who don't have direct involvement with students to administer the test in a professional manner. This includes social workers, psychologists, guidance counselors, department heads, administrators, or any educator available at the time needed. This will ensure the test is completed in a timely manner.

## Quashing the GPA

In this comprehensive plan, traditional grade point averages are replaced by a more effective indicator of school success. Of course, we don't give grades, but we also try to avoid averages. Here the number of students who have individual success is a stronger, more accurate indicator of the success of a school. Proficiency-based learning allows individual student gains in learning to be clearly documented. Rather than averages, the question now becomes: how many students made significant gains during the academic year?

Tracking the progress of students as individuals through demonstrated proficiencies rather than as a group allows for the gathering of very specific information. The results would read in different ways, they would be student specific. For example, John Jones demonstrated success in 18 of 25 proficiencies toward their learning goals. This improves his success rate by 8 percent over previous year.

Next, group success would be defined using a level playing field: sixty-two percent of the students made significant gains in their learning goals. Of course, "significant gains" would have to be defined by proficiencies completed, no matter what level those proficiencies were on. In taking students from "where they are," the most important thing is they are making significant gains as defined. A major effort in each school would be required to define a specific number of proficiencies needed for success. This would be indicated based on the student's specific action plan (MAP). Expectations would be held high by an overall norm for learning gains. An indicator of success is that the child gains at the rate expected in one year.

*Standards must become Learning Goals utilized as guidelines for success rather than deadlines for failure.*

Some might have a concern that one full year gain doesn't allow students to "catch up" to their peers. Consider this, children blossom in different ways and at different rates. Crediting author Susan Ohanian for recognizing children learn like sap from a maple tree, one drip at a time. Secondly, in the wealthier suburbs, where most students are on level, a "successful" school is expected to see increases of one year in reading. Why would it be different in urban schools?

Of course, we want students who are behind to gain more, that's what students do when we trade winning for learning. However, if schools bring a high percentage of students up by one level when in previous years those same students averaged 0.33 percent of a grade level gain, it is highly probable that the light went off and the student's level would continue to grow.

Remember, to bring students up to level, they must learn faster than the better students. This can be done, but one drip at a time.

## Proficiency Completion Rates

Moving on to high level achievement requires authentic, demonstrated assessments. This specific area will show a dramatic change from the past. For this process, an even playing field must be ensured for all to truly hold a school accountable through the assessment process.

By using authentic proficiencies, the caste system mentality has been removed. Every child is taken from "where they are" as schools are assessed on student's movement forward. Under this process, schools who serve the children who need the most will see individual achievement counted toward success in the form of the proficiency completion rate (PCR). The teachers who take on the challenge of the most troublesome children will be rewarded accordingly.

Every student will have a goal of completing specific proficiencies indicated in their MAP. A school will be held accountable for the number of students achieving that goal. For example, 74 percent of the students reached 85 percent of their proficiency goals. This PCR allows students to have high expectations that are challenging without catastrophic failure if they do not meet them. If they do meet their goals early, they aren't finished, the teacher simply raises the bar. Yes, the bar can be raised when it is individual. It is extremely important that this be monitored for fairness and high expectations.

## Parental Approval and Accessibility

Fundamental to any successful business is customer satisfaction. The same holds true for schools and should be included in their basic assessment. For this purpose, a satisfaction survey will be given to parents to provide their viewpoint on improving the school. This then becomes a tool of the overall assessment and accountability. A survey can be on paper, in person from the student, by phone or by e-mail or a combination of these. A sampling of this survey is as follows:

### Parent Satisfaction Survey

- Has your child's teacher responded to your concerns?
- Have you been treated fairly by your child's teacher?
- Has your child been treated fairly by all staff members?
- Have you been contacted by the teacher on a regular basis?
- Has the school philosophy been explained to you?

- Are you satisfied with your child's progress?
- Have you been contacted regarding school policy decisions?
- Do you feel school officials have listened to your concerns and ideas?
- Have you received a school calendar?
- Has school staff appropriately remedied school problems?
- Has the school lived up to your expectations?

## Teacher Satisfaction

Essential to implementing an effective school system is the ability for teachers to be able to teach and innovate at the highest level. With information from this survey, the school system will be altered to assure the full implementation of this new philosophy.

### *Teacher Satisfaction Survey*

- I have assurance that my curriculum meets the unique needs of all students.
- I have sufficient planning time.
- I have sufficient opportunity to participate in school development decisions.
- It is easy to connect my lessons to a strong overall school philosophy.
- I am satisfied as an educational professional.
- The school has supported my efforts to involve parents in their children's education.
- Community partners and other resources have been made available.
- I have sufficient opportunities to attend external professional development events.
- Class size is sufficient to meet students' needs.
- I receive full cooperation from administration.

## Student Satisfaction

The students play an integral part in the process of implementing the new philosophy. The time has come to become cognizant of the feelings of all students. Listening to them will allow many lessons to be learned.

- I feel teachers respect my feelings and opinions.
- I feel that my teachers want to help me learn.
- I feel comfortable asking my teachers questions and discussing problems I am having in class.
- I feel more motivated to learn new things.
- The kinds of things we do at this school and the way we learn makes me excited to come to school.

- Teachers talk with me often about how I am doing in class and how I can improve.
- I feel like I have had opportunities to give ideas for the classroom and school activities.
- My parents are more interested in my school work this year than before.

## School Environment

Schools will develop strategies at a fundamental level that create an environment conducive to learning:

- Team-building activities for both staff and students are planned and implemented, beginning before the first day of school. These activities continue throughout the school year as a vital part of the school curriculum.
- A well-planned, active curriculum is in place daily.
- All students are acknowledged for their success, no matter how small.
- Daily routine has students welcomed into school in a consistent manner.
- A plan is available to assure teachers are proactive in potential crises situations.
- Non-violent crises intervention workshops are made available.
- A student behavior plan/contract is created when necessary, by the teaching team, parents, and students. This connects with the students MAP as necessary. It is eliminated totally when successful.
- Peer mediation is made available.
- Character Development sessions are available to students.
- School behavior plans are designed to effectively use disciplinary action.
- Students are involved in developing the school rules.

## School Health and Safety

To secure the health and safety of all students, building maintenance must be reviewed on a regular basis.

- The school will assure all furnaces; air conditioners and other appliances are in safe working order.
- All doors and windows will be secure and in working order.
- The school will have all smoke alarms in working order.
- The school will assure all plumbing fixtures and electrical wiring is maintained on regular basis.
- The school will have a crisis plan in place including
  - A referral process for those who may need psychological support.

- ○ A training program designed to prepare teachers to recognize crises situations in students.
- ○ A lock down policy that secures the building without alarming students.
- ○ A telephone threat policy is in place.
- ○ An emergency phone in the office with an exclusive number is available.
- ○ A plan to notify parents of emergency situations. This will include by the media, by phone, by e-mail, or at a secure location in the school.

Essential to a successful school is a healthy environment, not only in the cafeteria, but throughout the school. Regular inspections must be held to assure this is maintained on an ongoing basis. In addition, policies that deal with student medications, blood, and liquid borne pathogens must be addressed. Remember Murphy's Law, anything that can happen, will happen.

- • The school will have regular inspections of cafeteria facilities to assure the highest health standards are maintained.
- • The school will provide regular inspections for pest control throughout the building.
- • The school will consult with nutrition experts to assure healthy meals are prepared for students.
- • The school will have healthy snacks available for students throughout the day.
- • The school will have a policy for students who receive medication at the school. This will include a secure location, a record indicating timely distribution as well as designated staff to issue said medications.
- • The school will keep medical records in a location accessible to staff members.
- • The school will provide training sessions as well as have proper materials for the safe handling of bodily fluids.

## Student Attendance

Essential to a successful school is to have students in school on a regular basis. Although there are many reasons for absenteeism, every effort should be made to partner with parents to come up with effective policies. The philosophy presented herein recognizes the differences in schools as well as in students.

It is important to recognize that schools have different students. For this reason, attendance data will not be valid to compare one school with another. However, an important part of the philosophy is that students are successful in their effort to learn meaningful information. Quality teaching and learning does not happen when the furniture is empty. Part of the success of this program is to make students and parents responsible for their presence in school on a timely basis.

Improvement in the attendance rate to a designated goal is a good indicator of the efforts of the school. The focus is on unexcused absences. An illness, family tragedy, or other legitimate reasons for absence are not directly affected by the school philosophy. The question to be assessed is not that of an average percentage. It is, however, that of the number of students meeting the goal, and the number of the students making gains in attendance throughout the year increases.

## Suspension Rates

Suspension rates are an indicator of the progress made in maintaining an environment conducive to learning, as well as the ability to appropriately support students in need. The number of students reaching the goal of no suspensions each year would be the information needed. In addition, the question relates to the improvement made by those who are suspended. It is important not to artificially refrain from suspension when needed. It is, however, important to solve the problem in the fastest way possible.

Utilizing as many resources as possible, every problematic child must be addressed as an individual. Of utmost concern is problems repeated on a regular basis. If suspensions are not resolving the problem, educators must look deeply into the issues surrounding the child. Not every problem can be resolved by the school, however, teaming with the parent and community, wrap around services might be able to make a difference.

Individual suspension rates must take priority and must be reduced for the school to be considered effective. A good indication may not be how many students are suspended, but how many have increased or reduced suspensions. Once this is tabulated, the issues can be more readily addressed.

## Dropout Rates

The question to be answered is this: of the students leaving the school, how many are graduating, dropping out, or choosing to go to a different school? Students remaining in a school are not considered a part of the equation. The school is shown to be successful when students complete, or when it is verified that they continue toward their completion in another program. Schools are not penalized as long as they support every student. When a student leaves a school, that school must follow them until they connect with a proper program. This leaves no cracks for the students to fall through. As long as students drop into a program, they are not dropouts.

Additional information must be gathered for students who leave the school and why they leave the school. This information will become a part of the accountability measure of a school. Any student "dumped" to another school, no matter what the reason, will be surveyed, holding the original school accountable when appropriate. An exception would be students whose family moves to another city or country, court actions, and any other movement outside of the control of the school. The following concerns must be addressed:

- The unacceptable move rate.
  ○ How many students left as unsatisfied customers?
  ○ How many students dropped out of school without dropping into another program?
  ○ How many students drop out due to low success rate (proficiency gains)?
  ○ How many students were removed for minor disciplinary reasons?
- What are acceptable reasons for removal?
  ○ Family moves out of the school's district or area.
  ○ Court action leading to mandated movement.
  ○ Movement to a school with a special academic focus when in line with student transition needs.

## Post-Secondary Placement Rates (PSPR)

To determine this rate, students who have completed their proficiencies for high school will be tracked to determine if they are enrolled in a post-secondary program or have begun a job. Post-secondary programs might include, but are not limited to, an internship, technical college, training facility, college, or university. Of the students who completed proficiency, how many are employed or have moved on to a higher level and completed that level? Notice the emphasis on "completed that level." Most can get into a university, for example, but the real issue is who succeeds at that university.

## MOVING FORWARD

This constitutes the new philosophy assessment process. These assessments are real, and they are valuable to ensure a quality school philosophy and design. In the past, the documentation had student gains strongly tied to time frames. Now that the playing field is level and students may gain skills at their own rate, student gains will be a fair indicator of their program.

Take the information presented in this book and make it your own. Our goal is to jump start whole child reform designed to take every child forward to their success. Together we can make miracles happen!

*When assessment is taken out of the realm of politics and a wide range of assessments are used for teachers and schools, only then, will they have value.*

## FOR CONTACT INFORMATION

## AND TO VISIT MY "SAVING STUDENTS BLOG" GO TO:

www.wholechildreform.com

# Bibliography

Allen, William Francis, Charles Pickard Ware, and Lucy McKim Garrison. *Slave Songs of the United States*. New York: Dover Publications, 1995.

Bridgeland, John, Dilulio, and Karen Burke Morison. *The Silent Epidemic: Perspectives of High School Drop Outs*. Washington, D.C.: Civic Enterprises with Peter D. Hart Research Associates for the Bill and Melinda Gates Foundation, 2006.

Budzisz, Mary Gale, and Eldon Lee. *Saving Students From A Shattered System*. Lanham, MD: Rowman & Littlefield Education, 2010.

Budzisz, Mary Gale, and Eldon Lee. *Quashing the Rhetoric of Reform*. Lanham, MD: Rowman & Littlefield Education, 2005.

Coalition for Community Schools. *System Failure*. New Orleans: Louisiana's Broken Charter School Law, The Center for popular democracy, 2015.

Dye, Dr. Angela. *The Phenomenon of Powerlessness and Student Achievement*. Minneapolis, MN: Capella University, 2014.

Dye, Dr. Angela. *Empowerment Starts Here*. Lanham, MD: Rowman & Littlefield Education, 2011.

England, Crystal. *Uphill Both Ways*. Portsmouth, NH: Heinemann, 2004.

Gardner, Dr. Howard. *Frames of Mind*. New York: Basic Books Inc., 1985.

Grandin, Temple. *Different ... Not Less*. Houston, TX: Future Horizons, 2012.

Gruwell, Erin. *The Freedom Writers Diary*. Long Beach, CA: The Freedom Writers Foundation, 2006.

Harvard Graduate School of Education. *Usable Knowledge, Connecting Research to Practice*. Cambridge, MA, 2017.

Hogan, Dan. *Science Daily*. www.sciencedaily.com. Rockville, MD, 2016.

Kolber, Jerry, and Bill Margol. *Brain Games*. National Geographic Channel, 2015.

Kozol, Jonathan. *Ordinary Resurrections*. New York: Crown Publishers.

Lee, Eldon. *Brainstorming Common Core*. Lanham, MD: Rowman & Littlefield Education, 2015.

Lucido, Horace. *Educational Genocide*. Lanham, MD: Rowman & Littlefield, 2010.

Marzano, Robert. *Designing and Teaching Learning Goals and Objectives.* Bloomington, IL: Marzano Research, 2009.

Meier, Deborah. *These Schools Belong to You and Me.* Boston: Beacon Press, 2017.

Merrow, John. *Merrow Report.* www.themerrowreport.com. New York, 2016.

Ohanian, Susan. *Caught in the Middle.* Portsmouth, NH: Heinemann, 2001.

Rutherford, Paula. *Why Didn't I learn This in College?* Alexandria, VA: Just Ask Publications and Professional Development, 2009.

Soundscapes.org. Popular Music and the Processes of Social Transformation, *Journal on Media Culture.* Groningen, the Netherlands: University of Groningen July 1999.

Tomlinson, Carol Ann. *The Differentiated Classroom.* Alexandria, VA: Association for Supervision and Development, 1999.

Tough, Paul. *How Children Succeed.* Boston: Houghton, Mifflin, Harcourt, 2012.

# Index

# About the Author

**Eldon "Cap" Lee** graduated from Eastern Michigan University and immediately headed to Milwaukee, Wisconsin, to pursue a career in education. His effort to teach students with special needs taught him that all children were different and had needs that must be met to assure a quality education. To expand his influence, he received his master's degree from Cardinal Stritch College and administrative certification from the University of Wisconsin, Milwaukee. He then took on the challenge of running an alternative school serving students with severe emotional problems. He culminated his career by developing the Milwaukee Village School, a fully public innovative school within the Milwaukee Public Schools. He continues to support innovative education.